Boho Baby Knits

groovy patterns for cool tots

Kat Coyle

PHOTOGRAPHY BY FRANK HECKERS

Illustrations by Marion Vitus

POTTER
CRAFT

New York

To my family,
Especially my son, Felix:
You make my world bright.

• • •

Copyright © 2007 by Quirk Packaging, Inc.

Published in the United States by Potter Craft, an imprint of the
Crown Publishing Group, a division of Random House, Inc., New York.
www.clarksonpotter.com
wwww.pottercraft.com

POTTER CRAFT and CLARKSON N. POTTER are trademarks, and
POTTER and colophon are registered trademarks of Random House, Inc.

Library of Congress Cataloging-in-Publication Data is available.

ISBN 978-0-307-38133-0

Printed in China

A QUIRK PACKAGING BOOK
Photography by Frank Heckers
Design by Lynne Yeamans
Layout by Nancy Leonard
Illustrations by Marion Vitus
Project management by Sarah Scheffel
Technical editing by Mandy Moore

10 9 8 7 6 5 4 3 2 1

First Edition

Contents
• • •

INTRODUCTION

• • •

Was your baby a regular at the neighborhood indie bookstore long before she learned her ABCs? Does the barista at your coffee bar automatically serve your little guy a steamed milk with a dash of cinnamon—just the way he likes it? Whether your kid is a beret-donning beatnik, a freewheeling musician, a moody poet, or a perfectly content Buddha-like baby, *Boho Baby Knits* contains patterns that'll outfit him for every occasion in style. Slurping at the café is always a joy when baby's wearing Bobbled Bloomers, and quiet time with a book is made even more memorable with the Story-time Socks. Art time is playtime with Petite Beat Bonnets, and you'll see that when your kid sports a Garage Band Tee, the concert always rocks.

The patterns are geared to discerning tots from four months to four years, and the designers (myself included) tried to bring a sense of humor and fun to each one. From the Folk Festival Frock and the Poet Coat to the Glam Rock Leggings and Beatnik Dolls, the offbeat looks and free-spirited attitudes of bohemians served as creative inspiration and guide. Our hope is that these distinctive knits will help nurture a spirit of individuality, imagination, and most of all fun in the kids who wear them (and the knitters, too!). Happily swathed in striking colors and snuggly yarns,

we can guarantee that the wearers of these garments will become used to admiring grown-ups remarking, "I want one for me!"

Picasso once said, "Every child is an artist. The problem is how to help him remain an artist once he grows up." Since the arrival of my own little boho, Felix, I've been inspired by his natural creativity. As I was designing and gathering ideas for this book, I paid attention to his drawings and stories. He was mad for aliens and ferocious lions. These went directly into Petite Beat Bonnets. His fascination with flying things meant he adored the knitted wings. And when I needed a model for a completed item, he would enthusiastically act the part of the poet or painter. The afternoon we had a tea party with the beatnik dolls, I felt confident other kids would love them as much as he did. Throughout the process his imagination fed mine.

I hope that knitting up these patterns will tap into your imaginative powers, too, and that you will have a great time along the way. Enjoy making the Big Idea Vest for your little philosopher, the Painter's Smock for your budding *artiste*, or Woodland Fairy Wings for your tiny visionary and watch as their imaginations take flight.

Kat Coyle

HOW TO USE THIS BOOK

• • •

This book assumes familiarity with basic knitting terms and techniques. The patterns range from challenging beginner patterns such as the Boho Boatneck and the Big Idea Vest; a variety of hat projects that might be completed over a weekend; and patterns that require more of your time and expertise (the Salon Set or Poet Coat, for example). If you're relatively new to knitting, don't worry: With more than thirty projects, accessories, and variations, it'll be easy to find patterns that are just right for you and your little boho.

Knitting terms used throughout the patterns are defined in the Abbreviations Chart here. I've also included a section called Stitch Story at the beginning of each pattern, which summarizes any special

Abbreviations Chart

• • •

CC, CC1, etc: contrasting colors

K: knit

K – or K0: this instruction does not apply to your size

K2tog or k3tog: decrease by knitting two (or three) stitches together as if they were one stitch

kfb: increase by knitting into the front and back of the next stitch

m1: insert the left needle, from back to front, under the horizontal strand that lies between the stitch just knit and the next stitch; knit this stitch through its front loop

MC: main color

P: purl

RS: right (public) side

S2KP: slip the next two stitches together knitwise (as if to k2tog), knit the next stitch, pass the slipped stitches over the stitch just knit—a double decrease

SKP: slip one stitch knitwise, knit the next stitch, pass the slipped stitch over—a single, left-slanting decrease

SK2P: slip one stitch knitwise, k2tog, pass the slip stitch over the stitch just made—a double decrease

sl: slip a stitch, purlwise, unless otherwise stated

ssk: decrease by slipping the next two stitches knitwise, one at a time, to the right needle, inserting the left needle into the fronts of these two stitches and knitting them together

sts: stitches

tbl: work the stitch through the back of the loop

WS: wrong side

YO: yarn over

( ): repeat the instructions in parentheses the number of times specified

* * repeat the instructions between the asterisks as described in the pattern

techniques used in the pattern and what you need to know to execute them. However, if a technique is completely new to you and you want to learn even more about it, see Useful Books and Websites, page 142.

Patterns for all ages, from newborns to four-year-olds, are included. However, it's best not to assume that your two-year-old will wear a size eighteen- to twenty-four-month sweater. In order to select the best pattern size for your child, first take his or her measurements and compare them to the ones provided under the finished measurements in the pattern. For tops, measure around the chest. Measure his or her waist and inseam if you're making pants, and around the head above the ears for hats. (Do not pull the tape measure tight; just let it sit comfortably around your little one.) Keep in mind that finished measurements in patterns include extra inches for ease, and a few of the styles such as the Big Idea Vest are oversized and meant to be loose.

Measuring clothes of a similar style that your child already owns can be helpful in gauging finished measurements in a pattern, too. If your kid is between sizes, you'll of course want to knit up, since by the time you've completed the project, he or she is likely to fill it out. If it's still loose when you're finished, that's cool: Your child will look that much more authentic as a hippy chick or grunge rocker.

I chose the beautiful yarns in this book for their rich palette and texture; all are of the highest quality (see Yarn Sources, page 142). Knitting with the best yarns makes all the time and effort required even more enjoyable. However, don't feel limited by my suggestions: If you want, you can experiment with other yarns to make these patterns your own. Just take care

to choose a yarn with the same weight and yardage of the yarn used in my sample, and check that your stitch gauge matches the one in the pattern.

A word on caring for these garments: Everyone knows that little bohos revel in their messiness—their creative lifestyles aren't fussy! Taking care of hand knits worn by creative kids will require extra attention, so wash them gently, use mild soaps, and lay them flat to dry. A few items in this book are worked in cotton yarns that can be laundered using the delicate cycle of the washing machine, but many are best served by hand washing. For best results, I suggest following the washing instructions found on the yarn label.

TODAY'S SPECIALS

Prankster's Poncho and Hat

Salon Set

Bloomsbury Nursing Shawl

Bobbled Bloomers and Toppers

Boho Boatneck

Mimi and Bobbi Beatnik Dolls

At the Café

Hang out at this stylish café where fresh and funky knits are on display. Budding conversationalists chat in style wearing the Salon Set, while up-and-coming trendsetters take tea with the irresistibly fashion-conscious Mimi and Bobbi Beatnik Dolls. Here *les petits bohémiens* chat with foamy milk mustaches, daydream, and scribble poems. Life is sweet!

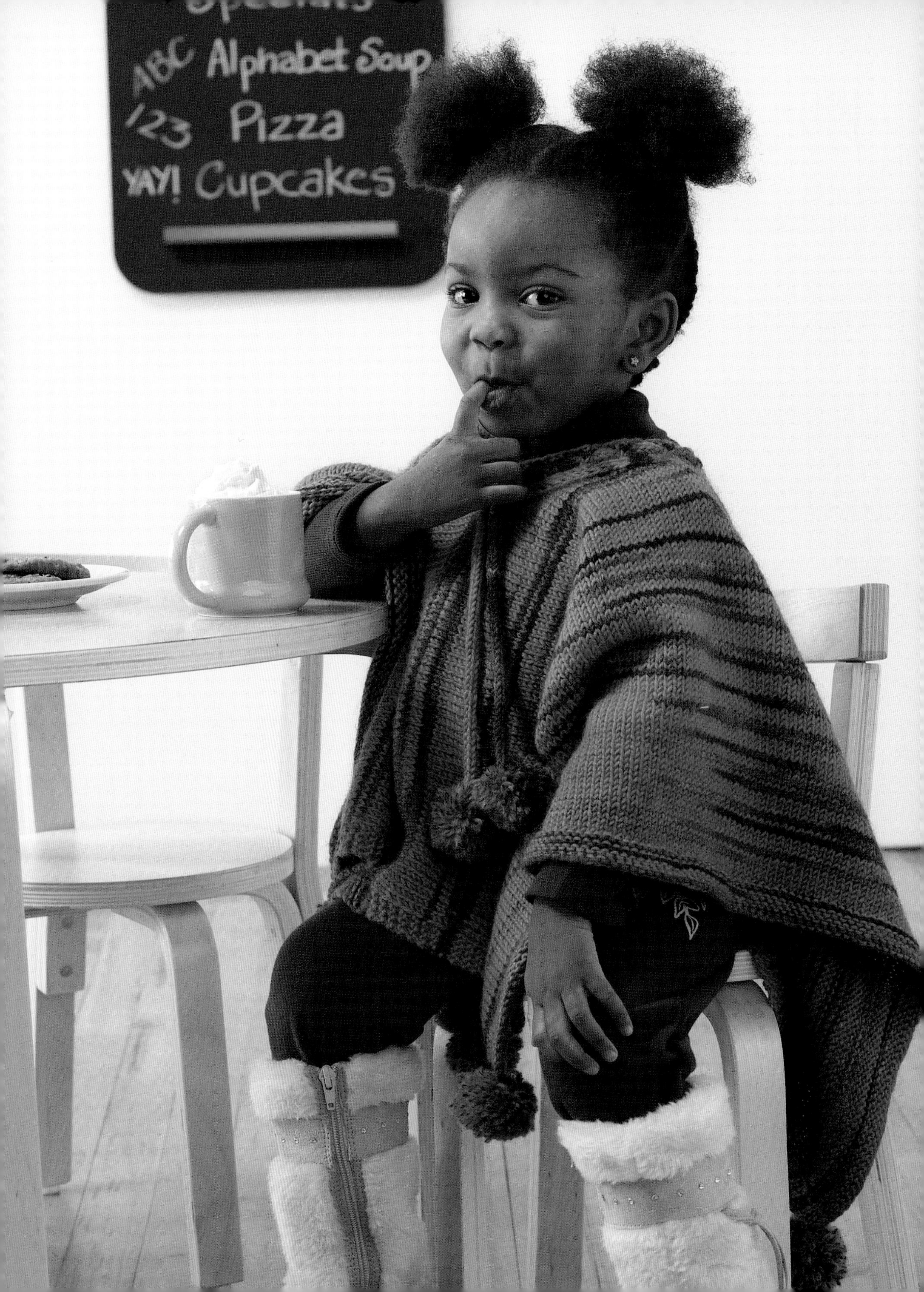
ABC Alphabet Soup
123 Pizza
YAY! Cupcakes

Prankster's Poncho and Hat

Your budding boho is sure to make mischief in this take on a traditional poncho. Inspired by a hand-woven serape, I chose a sophisticated self-striping yarn in turquoise wool with streaks of earth tones to mimic the richness of a woven pattern. The knitting is worked sideways, wrist to wrist, to create vertical striping. The neckline is finished with a sturdy I-cord drawstring; pom-poms complete the picture.

DESIGNED BY KAT COYLE

Finished Sizes and Measurements

• • •

1–2 years (2–3 years, 3–4 years)
Shown in size 2–3 years

PONCHO

Length from shoulder to hem:
13½ (15¼, 17¼)" (34.5 [38.5, 43.8]cm)

Width from edge of neck opening to wrist: 10 (11½, 12½)" (25.5 [29.2, 32]cm)

HAT

Circumference: 17 (18, 20)"
(43 [45.5, 51]cm)

Materials

• • •

Filatura Di Crosa 127 Print, 100% Wool, [93yd/85m per 50g skein]
Color: #36 Teal

Poncho: 6 (7, 9) balls

Hat: 1 (1, 2) balls

PONCHO

1 US #6 (4mm) circular needle, 24" (60cm) or longer

1 US #7 (4.5mm) circular needle, 24" (60cm) or longer

2 spare circular needles, US #7 (4.5mm) or smaller, 24" (60cm) or longer

One 16" (40cm) US #7 (4.5mm) circular needle

1 set US #6 (4mm) double-pointed needles

HAT

1 US #7 (4.5mm) circular needle (any length) or set of straight needles

Stitch marker

Tapestry needle

2" (5cm) pom-pom maker

Gauge

• • •

19 stitches and 25 rows = 4" (10cm) in stockinette stitch using US #7 (4.5 mm) needles

SK2P (Slip 1, K2tog, Pass slipped stitch over): Slip the next stitch knitwise, knit 2 together, pass the slipped stitch over the stitch just worked.

THREE-NEEDLE BIND-OFF

Hold both pieces of knitting with right sides together. Insert needle into the first stitch on the front needle and first stitch on the back needle, and knit them together. *Repeat this for the next stitch on the front and back needles. Draw the first stitch worked over the second stitch.*
Repeat from * to * until all stitches have been bound off. Cut the yarn and draw it through the remaining stitch.

I-CORD

Using a double-pointed needle, cast on 3 stitches.
Next Row: Instead of turning the work around to work back on the wrong side, slide all stitches to the other end of the needle, transfer the needle to your left hand, bring the yarn around the back of the work, and start knitting the stitches again.
I-Cord is worked with the right side facing you at all times.
Repeat this row to form I-cord. After a few rows, the work will begin to form a tube.

• • •

PONCHO

• • •

Note: *When working this pattern, the first stitch of each row is slipped knitwise to give a neat edge.*

Each half of the Poncho is cast on at the side edge and is worked toward the center. Once both halves have been worked, they are joined using a three-needle bind-off.

RIGHT HALF

• •

Using a US #6 (4mm) circular needle, cast on 128 (144, 164) stitches.
Knit 6 rows, slipping the first stitch of each row.

Row 1 (RS): Using the longer US #7 (4.5mm) circular needle, work as follows: Sl 1, knit to end.
Row 2 (WS): Sl 1, k3, purl to last 4 stitches, k4.
Repeat these 2 rows until work measures 10 (11½, 12½)" (25.5 [29.2, 32]cm), ending with a wrong side row.

SHAPE NECK OPENING

• •

Next Row (RS): Sl 1, k58 (66, 76), k3tog, k2. Place remaining stitches on hold on a spare circular needle. 62 (70, 80) stitches.

Right Front
Row 1 (WS): P to last 4 stitches, k4.
Row 2 (RS): Sl 1, knit to last 5 stitches, k3tog, k2. Repeat these 2 rows 6 (7, 7) times more, then work Row 1 once more. 48 (54, 64) stitches. Place all stitches on hold on a spare circular needle. Cut the yarn, leaving a tail approximately 63 (70, 84)" (160 [178, 214]cm) long.

Right Back
Slip held stitches (from beginning of neck shaping) to the US #7 (4.5mm) circular needle, with the right side facing, and rejoin the yarn.

Row 1 (RS): K2, SK2P, knit to end.
Row 2 (WS): Sl 1, k3, purl to end.
Repeat these 2 rows 7 (8, 8) times more. 48 (54, 64) stitches. Place all stitches on hold on a spare circular needle. Cut the yarn, leaving a tail approximately 63 (70, 84)" (160 [178, 214]cm) long.

LEFT HALF

· ·

Work the same as the
right half. Make the left back the
same way as the right front. Make
the left front the same way as the
right back.

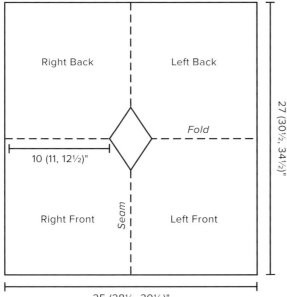

Place the stitches of the left back on hold on the
US #6 (4mm) circular needle while the left front
is being worked. When the left front is complete,
do not remove it from the working needle.

Finishing

· · ·

Hold the two halves with their right sides together.
Use the long yarn tails and the three-needle bind off
to join the right and left fronts together, then join the
right and left backs in the same way.

Weave in all ends.
Immerse the Poncho in lukewarm water and allow
it to soak until it is thoroughly saturated. Gently
squeeze out the water (do not wring!) and lay the
Poncho on top of several towels on a flat surface.
Carefully pin it out to the dimensions given. Allow
it to dry completely.

Right Back	Left Back

10 (11, 12½)"

Fold

Seam

Right Front	Left Front

27 (30½, 34½)"

25 (28½, 30½)"

NECKBAND

Using the shorter US #7 (4.5mm) circular needle, beginning at the center back of the neck opening, pick up and knit 1 stitch for each row and 1 stitch in each corner around the opening. You should have 76 (80, 80) stitches; if you do not, increase or decrease as necessary to achieve the correct number. Place marker and join to begin working in the round.

Round 1: *K2, p2, repeat from * to end.
Round 2: *K2tog, yo, repeat from * to end.
Round 3: Work as for Round 1.
Bind off all stitches loosely.

DRAWSTRING

Using double-pointed needles, work a 36 (38, 42)" (91 [96.5, 106.5]cm) length of I-Cord. When I-Cord is complete, cut the yarn, draw it through all stitches on the needle, and pull tight.

POM-POMS

Use the pom-pom maker to make 6 Pom-Poms. Sew one to each end of the drawstring, and one to each corner of the Poncho.

HAT

Using US #7 (4.5mm) needles, cast on 50 (52, 57) stitches. Leave a long yarn tail at the beginning of your cast-on; it can be used later when sewing the Hat together.

Row 1 (WS): Sl 1, k3, purl to last 4 stitches, k4.
Row 2 (RS): Sl 1, knit to end.
Repeat these 2 rows until work measures 8½ (9, 10)" (21.5 [23, 55.5]cm), ending with a wrong side row. Bind off all stitches, leaving a long yarn tail at the end of the bind-off.

Finishing

Fold the Hat in half, so that the side edges of the work meet. Use the yarn tails to sew the two halves of the cast-on edge together. Sew the two halves of the bound-off edge together in the same way.

Use the pom-pom maker to make 2 Pom-Poms, and sew one to each corner of the hat.

Weave in all ends.

Salon Set

This festive skirt with a petticoat hem reminds me of the ruffled skirts that I wore for folk dancing performances in grammar school. Knit in a shiny mercerized cotton, it looks as cheerful and crisp as the geraniums we pinned in our hair. The skirt is worked in the round from the top down. The waistband is knit together with the skirt, and the lace edging is knit to the live skirt stitches. The hat is also worked in the round, with a lacy pinwheel design at its crown.

DESIGNED BY KAT COYLE

Finished Sizes and Measurements

• • •

1–2 years (2–3 years, 3–4 years)
Shown in size 1–2 years

SKIRT

Waist circumference *(after elastic insertion)*: 18 (19, 20)" (45.5 [48.5, 51]cm)

Length: 10¾ (11¾, 13¼)" (27.3 [29.8, 33.5]cm)

HAT

Circumference: 18¼" (46.4cm)
One size will fit most toddlers

Materials

• • •

Tahki Cotton Classic, 100% Mercerized Cotton, [108 yd/99m per 50g skein]
Color: #3911 Magenta

Skirt: 3 (4, 5) skeins

Hat: 1 skein

1 set US #6 (4mm) double-pointed needles

One 16" (40cm) US #5 (3.75mm) circular needle (skirt only)

One 16" (40cm) US #6 (4mm) circular needle

One 24" (60cm) US #6 (4mm) circular needle

1 crochet hook (for crochet cast-on only)

Waste yarn

Stitch markers

Yarn needle

1 package 1" (25mm) waistband elastic

Sewing needle and white thread to sew elastic band together

Gauge

• • •

21 stitches and 29 rows = 4" (10cm) in stockinette stitch using US #6 (4mm) needle

Lace edging is 3¼" (8.3cm) wide

S2KP (Slip 2, Knit 1, Pass slipped stitch over): Slip the next 2 stitches together, knitwise, as if to work a k2tog. Knit the next stitch, then pass both slipped stitches together over the stitch just knit. This forms a centered double decrease.

M1L (Make 1 Left): Insert the left needle, from front to back, under the horizontal strand that lies between the stitch just knit and the next stitch. Knit this stitch through its back loop.

M1R (Make 1 Right): Insert the left needle, from back to front, under the horizontal strand that lies between the stitch just knit and the next stitch. Knit this stitch through its front loop.

CROCHET CAST-ON

Using waste yarn, work a crochet chain several stitches longer than the number of stitches to be cast on. Starting 1 or 2 stitches in from the end of the chain and using the working yarn, pick up and knit 1 stitch in the back loop of each chain stitch until the required number of stitches have been worked. Later, the chain will be unraveled and the resulting live stitches picked up.

• • •

SKIRT

• • •

Using US #5 (3.75mm) circular needle and crochet cast-on, cast on 120 (128, 132) stitches, leaving a 6" (15cm) yarn tail. Do not join.
Work 8 rows in stockinette stitch, beginning with a wrong side row.
With the right side facing, place a stitch marker and join to begin working in the round, being careful not to twist the stitches.
Purl 1 round. This round forms a turning ridge for the waistband elastic casing.
Using the shorter US #6 (4mm) circular needle, knit 8 rounds.

Remove the crochet chain from the cast-on edge, and place the resulting live stitches on the US #5 (3.75mm) circular needle. Fold the work along the turning ridge so that the wrong sides are together, with the stitches of the cast-on edge held behind the stitches on the working needle.

Next Round: *Knit the first stitch on the working needle together with the first stitch of the cast-on edge; repeat from * until all stitches have been worked. The waistband is complete.

Set-Up Round: K30 (32, 33), place marker, k60 (64, 66), place marker, knit to end.
These markers indicate the center front and center back of the Skirt.

Increase Round: *Knit to 1 stitch before marker, M1R, k2, M1L, repeat from * once, knit to end. 4 stitches increased.
Knit 1 round.
Repeat these 2 rounds 14 times more, switching to the longer circular needle when necessary. 180 (188, 192) stitches.

Work Increase Round.
Knit 3 rounds.
Repeat these 4 rounds 1 (3, 5) times more. 188 (204, 216) stitches.

Continue in stockinette stitch until the work measures 6 (7, 8½)" (15 [18, 21.5]cm) from the set-up round. Cut the yarn.

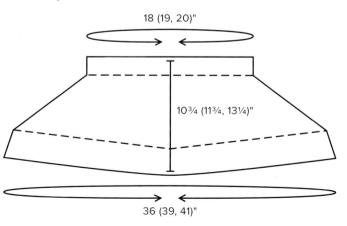

18 (19, 20)"

10¾ (11¾, 13¼)"

36 (39, 41)"

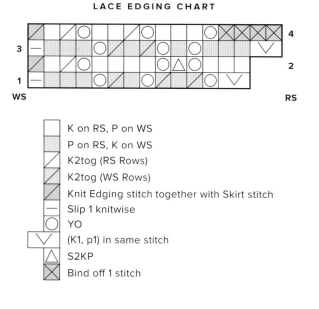

Using a double-pointed needle, cast on 13 stitches. Work Row 1 of the Lace Edging, working the Edging onto the needle that holds the Skirt stitches, with the wrong side of the Skirt facing. Work the Lace Edging, attaching the Edging to the lower edge of the Skirt as indicated, until only 1 Skirt stitch remains.
Work Row 3 of the Lace Edging.
Bind off all stitches of the Edging, working the last stitch of the Edging together with the last Skirt stitch. Cut the yarn, leaving a 12" (30.5cm) tail. Use this tail to sew the ends of the Edging together.

Finishing

● ● ●

Cut a piece of waistband elastic 18 (19, 20)" (45.5 [48.5, 51]cm) long, or 1" (2.5cm) shorter than waist measurement. Insert the elastic into the waistband casing, ensuring that it does not twist. Overlap the ends of the elastic by 1" (2.5cm), and use the needle and thread to securely sew the ends together. Use the yarn tail remaining from the cast-on to sew the casing closed.

Weave in all ends.
Immerse the Skirt in lukewarm water and allow it to soak until it is thoroughly saturated. Gently squeeze out the water (do not wring!) and lay it on top of several towels on a flat surface. Carefully pin out the points of the Lace Edging. Allow the Skirt to dry completely.

HAT

● ● ●

Using the shorter US #6 (4mm) circular needle, cast on 96 stitches. Place a marker and join to begin working in the round, being careful not to twist the stitches.
Work in stockinette stitch until the work measures 5" (12.5cm).

Switching to double-pointed needles when necessary, shape the crown as follows:
Round 1: *Ssk, k12, k2tog, yo, repeat from * 5 times, ssk, k12, k2tog. 89 stitches.
Round 2: Yo, knit to end. 90 stitches.

LACE EDGING

● ●

Cast on 13 stitches.
Row 1 (WS): Sl 1 knitwise, k3, *yo, k2tog, k1, repeat from * once, k2tog, yo, (k1, p1) in last stitch. 14 stitches.
Row 2 (RS): K3, yo, S2KP, yo, k4, yo, k2tog, k1, knit last stitch together with next stitch of Skirt.
Row 3 (WS): Sl 1 knitwise, k3, yo, k2tog, k1, k2tog, yo, k1, yo, k3, (k1, p1) in last stitch. 16 stitches.
Row 4 (RS): Bind off 4 stitches, yo, k3, yo, k2tog, k2, yo, k2tog, k1, knit last stitch together with next stitch of Skirt. 13 stitches.
Repeat Rows 1–4 for Lace Edging.

LACE EDGING CHART

	K on RS, P on WS
	P on RS, K on WS
/	K2tog (RS Rows)
\	K2tog (WS Rows)
	Knit Edging stitch together with Skirt stitch
—	Slip 1 knitwise
○	YO
∨	(K1, p1) in same stitch
△	S2KP
⊠	Bind off 1 stitch

Round 3: *K1, ssk, k10, k2tog, yo, repeat from * 5 times, k1, ssk, k10, k2tog. 83 stitches.

Round 4: Yo, knit to end. 84 stitches.

Round 5: *K2, ssk, k8, k2tog, yo, repeat from * 5 times, k2, ssk, k8, k2tog. 77 stitches.

Round 6: Yo, knit to end. 78 stitches.

Round 7: *K3, ssk, k6, k2tog, yo, repeat from * 5 times, k3, ssk, k6, k2tog. 71 stitches.

Round 8: Yo, knit to end. 72 stitches.

Round 9: *K4, ssk, k4, k2tog, yo, repeat from * 5 times, k4, ssk, k4, k2tog. 65 stitches.

Round 10: Yo, knit to end. 66 stitches.

Round 11: *K5, ssk, k2, k2tog, yo, repeat from * 5 times, k5, ssk, k2, k2tog. 59 stitches.

Round 12: Yo, knit to end. 60 stitches.

Round 13: *K6, ssk, k2tog, yo, repeat from * to end. 54 stitches.

Round 14: Knit to last 2 stitches. Slip these stitches to the right needle and remove the marker, slip them back to the left needle and replace the marker. This point is now the beginning of the round.

Round 15: *Ssk, k5, k2tog, yo, repeat from * to end. 48 stitches.

Round 16: Knit all stitches.

Round 17: *Ssk, k3, k2tog, yo, k1, repeat from * to end. 42 stitches.

Round 18: Knit all stitches.

Round 19: *Ssk, k1, k2tog, yo, k2, repeat from * to end. 36 stitches.

Round 20: Knit all stitches.

Round 21: *S2KP, yo, k3, repeat from * to end. 30 stitches.

Round 22: Knit to last stitch, slip last stitch to the right needle, remove marker, slip stitch back to the left needle and replace the marker.

Round 23: *S2KP, yo, k2, repeat from * to end. 24 stitches.

Round 24: Knit to last stitch, slip last stitch to the right needle, remove marker, slip stitch back to the left needle and replace the marker.

Round 25: *S2KP, k1, repeat from * 5 times, S2KP, slip last stitch to the right needle, remove marker, slip stitch back to the left needle and replace the marker. 12 stitches.

Round 26: K2tog 6 times. Cut the yarn, leaving a 6" (15cm) tail. Draw this tail through the remaining 6 stitches and pull tight.

Finishing

• • •

Weave in all ends.

Immerse the Hat in lukewarm water and allow it to soak until it is thoroughly saturated. Gently squeeze out the water (do not wring!) and lay on top of several towels on a flat surface. Allow the lower edge to roll slightly. Dry completely.

• • •

Bloomsbury Nursing Shawl

When I nursed Felix in public, I preferred to use a small blanket or shawl as a cover. Textured without being bulky, this petite shawl is perfect for nursing and does double-duty as a baby blanket, too. I chose an easy-care yarn in deep olive, pink, and lilac. The lace motifs and garden colors remind me of the decorative style of the Bloomsbury artists. The knitted fringe serves as an elastic and ornamental bind-off.

DESIGNED BY KAT COYLE

Finished Measurements

• • •

Length: 47" (119.5cm)

Width: 23" (58.5cm)

Note: Measurements given for after blocking.

Materials

• • •

Rowan Wool Cotton, 50% Merino Wool / 50% Cotton, [123 yds/113 m per 50g ball]
Colors:
[MC] #907 Deepest Olive; 6 balls
[CC1] #943 Flower; 2 balls
[CC2] #954 Grand; 1 ball

1 US #6 (4mm) circular needle, 24" (60cm) or longer

1 spare circular needle, US #6 (4mm) or smaller, 24" (60cm) or longer

1 crochet hook (for crochet cast-on only)

Waste yarn

Blunt yarn needle

Rust-proof pins (for blocking)

Stitch markers (optional)

1 x ⅝" (15mm) button (optional)

Sewing needle and thread to match olive green yarn (optional)

Gauge

• • •

23 stitches and 29 rows = 4" (10cm) in Checks pattern, before blocking

19 stitches and 29 rows = 4" (10cm) in Checks pattern, after blocking

• • • STITCH STORY • • •

S2KP (Slip 2, Knit 1, Pass slipped stitch over): Slip the next 2 stitches together, knitwise, as if to work a k2tog. Knit the next stitch, then pass both slipped stitches over the stitch just knit. This forms a centered double decrease.

K4tog: Knit 4 together (3 stitches decreased).

K4tog tbl: Knit 4 together through back loops (3 stitches decreased).

CROCHET CAST-ON

Using waste yarn, work a crochet chain several stitches longer than the number of stitches to be cast on. Starting 1 or 2 stitches in from the end of the chain and using the working yarn, pick up and knit 1 stitch in the back loop of each chain stitch until the required number of stitches have been worked. Later, the chain will be unraveled and the resulting live stitches picked up.

KNITTED CAST-ON

*Insert the right needle into the first stitch on the left needle. Wrap the yarn and draw it through the stitch as if to knit, but do not remove the old stitch from the left needle. Slip the new stitch from the right needle to the left needle.

Repeat from * for each new stitch to be cast on.

GRAFTING

Place the two pieces flat with right sides up, so that the edges with live stitches are nearly touching. Position yourself so that the piece that is attached to the yarn tail is farthest from you. Thread the yarn tail onto a blunt yarn needle.

*Beginning with the stitches on the needle closest to you, insert the needle down into the first stitch, then up through the second stitch. Slide the first stitch off the needle. Working into the stitches on the needle farthest from you, insert the needle down into the first stitch, then up through the second stitch. Slide the first stitch off the needle.

Repeat from * until all stitches have been worked. Every few stitches, adjust the tension of the grafted stitches so that it matches the tension of the rest of the work.

• • •

SHAWL

• • •

Note: If you are new to lace knitting, you may wish to place a stitch marker after each repeat of the stitch pattern to help you keep track.

FIRST HALF

• •

Using the crochet cast-on method and MC, cast on 109 stitches.

Rows 1–8: Using MC, work Rows 1–8 of the Shell Chart.
Rows 9–10: Using CC2, work Rows 9–10 of the Shell Chart.
Rows 11–18: Using CC1, work Rows 1–8 of the Checks Chart.

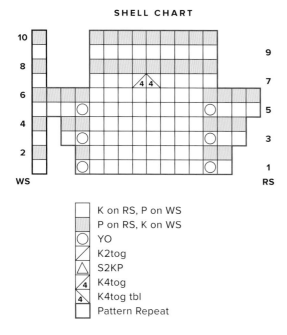

SHELL CHART

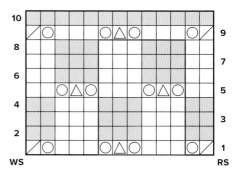

CHECKS CHART

☐	K on RS, P on WS
▨	P on RS, K on WS
◯	YO
╱	K2tog
△	S2KP
4╱	K4tog
4╲	K4tog tbl
☐	Pattern Repeat

Rows 19–20: Using CC2, work Rows 9–10 of the Checks Chart.

Rows 21–28: Using MC, Work Rows 1–8 of the Shell Chart.

Rows 29–30: Using CC1, work Rows 9–10 of the Shell Chart.

Rows 31–38: Using CC2, work Rows 1–8 of the Checks Chart.

Rows 39–40: Using CC1, work Rows 9–10 of the Checks Chart.

Rows 41–60: Work as for Rows 1–20.

Rows 61–172: Using MC, work Rows 1–8 of the Checks Chart 14 times. Cut the yarn and slip all stitches to a spare circular needle.

SECOND HALF

Rows 1–172: Work as for First Half.

Rows 173–175: Work Rows 1–3 of the Checks Chart. Cut the yarn, leaving a tail approximately 3 yds (3m) long.

Use this yarn tail to graft the First and Second Halves together.

FRINGE

Remove the crochet chain from one cast-on end of the Shawl and place the resulting live stitches on the needle with the wrong side facing.

Using CC1, purl 1 row.

Next Row (RS): Bind off 1 stitch, *slip the stitch on the right needle to the left needle, cast on 5 stitches using the knitted cast-on, bind off 8 stitches, repeat from * until all stitches have been bound off.

Repeat on second cast-on edge.

Finishing

Weave in all ends.

Immerse the Shawl in lukewarm water and allow it to soak until it is thoroughly saturated. Gently squeeze out the water (do not wring!) and lay the Shawl on top of several towels on a flat surface. Carefully pin it out to the dimensions given. (If desired, the Shawl can be stretched out at this point and pinned out to larger dimensions, which will give a more open, lacy effect.) Allow it to dry completely.

If desired, sew a button near the edge of the Shawl, approximately 15" (38cm) from one cast-on end. When fastening the Shawl, use one of the holes that result from the lace pattern as a buttonhole.

Tea Party!!
Cranberry Scones
Crumpets · Jam
Tarts

Bobbled Bloomers and Toppers

For natural mommies, wool "soakers" are a must-have to keep cloth diapers from leaking, but these cuties will look good on any baby's booty. Fancy up baby's bottom with some striped and bobbled bloomers—and make the coordinating topper for extra kicks. Use the colors of your choice to make the set. The topper uses the same yarn and stitch work as the bloomer, with a switch in the order of colors.

DESIGNED BY KAT COYLE

Finished Sizes and Measurements

• • •

0–6 months (6–12 months, 12–24 months)

Shown in size 0–6 months [Colorway A] and size 6–12 months [Colorway B]

BLOOMERS

Hip circumference: 14½ (16¾, 19¼)" (37 [42.5, 50.3]cm)

HAT

Circumference: 14½ (15½, 16¾)" (37 [39.5, 42.5]cm)

Materials

• • •

Cascade Yarns Cascade 220 Quatro, 100% Wool, [220yd/201m per 100g skein], 1 skein of each color will make both Bloomers and Topper

COLORWAY A

[MC] #9440 Red/Purple

[CC1] #9433 Red/Pink

[CC2] #9438 Pink/Peach

COLORWAY B

[MC] #9435 Light green/Dark green

[CC1] #9439 Lavender/Green

[CC2] #9437 Purple/Lavender

1 set US #6 (4mm) double-pointed needles

1 set US #7 (4.5mm) double-pointed needles (Topper only)

One 16" (40cm) US #7 (4.5mm) circular needle

Stitch holders

Yarn needle

Gauge

• • •

20 stitches and 24 rows = 4" (10cm) in stockinette stitch, using US #7 (4.5mm) needle

1x1 rib (Worked in the round over an even number of stitches):
Round 1: *K1, p1, repeat from * to end.
Repeat this round for 1x1 rib.

MB (Make Bobble): (Knit into the front, then back, then front, then back, then front again) of the next stitch: 1 stitch increased to 5 stitches.
*Turn work, k5. Turn work, p5. Repeat from * once more.
Slip second, third, fourth, and fifth stitches over first stitch, then knit this stitch. 1 stitch remains; bobble is complete.

THREE-NEEDLE BIND-OFF
Hold both pieces of knitting with right sides together. Insert the needle into the first stitch on the front needle and first stitch on the back needle, and knit them together. *Repeat this for the next stitch on the front and back needles. Draw the first stitch worked over the second stitch.*
Repeat from * to * until all stitches have been bound off. Cut yarn and draw through remaining stitch.

• • •

BLOOMERS
• • •

Begin with waistband.
Using US #6 (4mm) double-pointed needles and MC, cast on 72 (84, 96) stitches. Divide stitches between needles and join to begin working in the round, being careful not to twist the stitches.
Work in 1x1 rib until the work measures 3 (3½, 3¾)" (7.5 [9, 9.5]cm).

Switch to circular needle and CC1, and knit 6 (8, 10) rounds.
Using MC, knit 1 round, then purl 1 round.
Next Round: Using CC2, *k5, MB, repeat from * to end.
Using CC2, knit 1 round.
Using MC, knit 1 round, then purl 1 round.
Using CC1, knit 6 (8, 10) rounds.

SHAPE LEG OPENINGS
• •

Using MC, knit 1 round. Turn work so that wrong side is facing.

FRONT
• •

Row 1 (WS): Using MC, k36 (42, 48), slip remaining stitches to a stitch holder for Back.
Row 2 (RS): Using CC2, sl 1, k1, ssk, k1, MB, *k5, MB, repeat from * to last 6 stitches, k2, k2tog, k2. 34 (40, 46) stitches.
Row 3 (WS): Using CC2, sl 1, purl to end.

Row 4 (RS): Using MC, sl 1, k1, ssk, knit to last 4 stitches, k2tog, k2. 32 (38, 44) stitches.

Row 5 (WS): Using MC, sl 1, knit to end.

Row 6 (RS): Using CC1, sl 1, k1, ssk, knit to last 4 stitches, k2tog, k2.

Row 7 (WS): Using CC1, sl 1 purl to end.

Repeat Rows 6 and 7, 2 (3, 4) times more. 26 (30, 34) stitches.

Next Row (RS): Using MC, sl 1, k1, ssk, knit to last 4 stitches, k2tog, k2. 24 (28, 32) stitches.

Next Row (WS): Using MC, sl 1, knit to end.

Work Rows 2–5 as above. 20 (24, 28) stitches.

Sizes 6–12 months and 12–24 months only: Work Rows 6–7 – (2, 3) times. – (20, 22) stitches.

All Sizes:

Slipping the first stitch of each row, continue as follows:

Using CC1, work 6 (4, 4) rows in stockinette stitch.

Using MC, knit 2 rows.

Using CC2, work 2 rows in stockinette stitch.

Using MC, knit 2 rows.

Using CC1, work 3 (5, 5) rows in stockinette stitch.

Cut the yarn and place all stitches on a stitch holder.

BACK

Replace the held stitches of the Back on the needle with the wrong side facing, reattach MC, and knit 1 row.

Slipping the first stitch of each row and working stripes and bobbles as for Front, shape Back as follows:

Work 12 (14, 12) rows in pattern.

Decrease Row (RS): Sl 1, k1, ssk, knit to last 4 stitches, k2tog, k2.

Work 1 row in pattern.

Repeat these 2 rows 7 (10, 12) times more. 20 (20, 22) stitches.

Work 5 (3, 5) rows in stockinette stitch.

Place the held stitches of the Front on a double-pointed needle. Join Front and Back stitches using the three-needle bind-off.

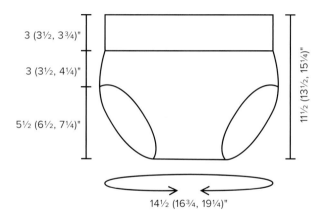

3 (3½, 3¾)"

3 (3½, 4¼)"

5½ (6½, 7¼)"

11½ (13½, 15¼)"

14½ (16¾, 19¼)"

LEG BANDS

• •

Using US #6 (4mm) double-pointed needles and MC, pick up and knit stitches around one leg opening as follows:

For sizes 0–6 months and 6–12 months, pick up and knit 2 stitches for every 3 rows.

For size 12–24 months, pick up and knit 3 stitches for every 4 rows.

You will have 44 (52, 64) stitches. Join to begin working in the round.

Work in 1x1 rib until cuff measures 2½ (3, 3½)" (6.5 [7.5, 9]cm).

Loosely bind off all stitches in pattern.

Finishing

• • •

Weave in all ends.

TOPPER

• • •

Using US #6 (4mm) double-pointed needles and CC2, cast on 72 (78, 84) stitches.

Divide stitches among needles and join to begin working in the round, being careful not to twist the stitches.

Work in 1x1 rib until the work measures 3 (3¼, 3½)" (7.5 [8.3, 9]cm).

Using circular needle and CC1, knit 6 (8, 10) rounds.
Using CC2, knit 1 round, then purl 1 round.
Next Round: Using MC, *k5, MB, repeat from * to end.
Using MC, knit 1 round.
Using CC2, knit 1 round, then purl 1 round.

Repeat the last 12 (12, 14) rounds once. *(Note: Sizes 6–12 months and 12–24 months will only work 6 [8] rounds in CC1 before repeating the stripe sequence, instead of 8 [10] rounds.)*

Using CC1, knit 6 (6, 8) rounds.

Switching to US #7 (4.5mm) double-pointed needles when necessary, shape crown as follows:

Round 1: Using CC2, *k4, k2tog, repeat from * to end. 60 (65, 70) stitches.

Round 2: Using CC2, purl all stitches.

Round 3: Using MC, *k4, MB, repeat from * to end.

Round 4: Using MC, knit all stitches.

Round 5: Using CC2, *k3, k2tog, repeat from * to end. 48 (52, 56) stitches.

Round 6: Using CC2, purl all stitches.

Round 7: Using CC1, *k2, k2tog, repeat from * to end. 36 (39, 42) stitches.

Continue with CC1 to end.

Round 8: Knit all stitches.

Round 9: *K1, k2tog, repeat from * to end. 24 (26, 28) stitches.

Round 10: Knit all stitches.

Round 11: *K2tog, repeat from * to end. 12 (13, 14) stitches.

Cut the yarn, leaving a tail approximately 6 inches long. Draw this tail through the remaining stitches and pull tight.

Finishing

• • •

Weave in all ends.

• • •

Boho Boatneck

In this story of the café life, we might cast the resident artist in this long-sleeved boatneck. He's the neighborhood's celebrity painter, whose recent successes have led to a habit of perusing the financial news. No matter who wears it, this sweater's bright stripes make the scene. Simple to knit in supple, soft cotton, the look is casual and comfy for your kid to lounge in.

DESIGNED BY EDNA HART

Finished Sizes and Measurements

• • •

12–18 months (18–24 months, 2–3 years, 3–4 years)
Shown in size 18–24 months
Chest: 22 (24, 26, 28)" (56 [61, 66, 71]cm)
Length: 11 (12, 14, 15)" (28 [30.5, 35.5, 38]cm)

Materials

• • •

Manos del Uruguay Cotton Stria, 100% Cotton, [116 yd/106m per 50g skein]; 1 (1, 1, 2) hanks each color

[MC] #216 Navy
[CC1] #212 Light Blue
[CC2] #218 Yellow
[CC3] #206 Orange

1 set US #7 (4.5mm) straight needles

Yarn needle

Gauge

• • •

18 stitches and 28 rows = 4" (10cm) in stockinette stitch

• • • STITCH STORY • • •

STRIPE SEQUENCE
2 Rows MC (Navy)
2 Rows CC1 (Light Blue)
2 Rows CC2 (Yellow)
4 Rows CC3 (Orange)
Repeat these 10 rows for stripe sequence.

• • •

BOATNECK

• • •

BACK

• •

Using MC, cast on 50 (54, 58, 64) stitches.

Row 1 (RS): K2 (2, 2, 3), *p2, k2, repeat from * to last 0 (0, 0, 1) stitches, k0 (0, 0, 1).

Row 2 (WS): P2 (2, 2, 3), *k2, p2, repeat from * to last 0 (0, 0, 1) stitches, p0 (0, 0, 1). Cut MC.

Row 3 (RS): Using CC1, work as for Row 1.

Work in stockinette stitch, continuing in stripe sequence, until work measures 10¾ (11¾, 13¾, 14¾)" (27.3 [29.8, 34.9, 37.5]cm), ending with a right side row. *(**Note:** You might not end on the last row of the stripe pattern.)*

Knit 2 rows using MC.
Bind off all stitches.

FRONT

• •

Work as for Back.

SLEEVES (MAKE 2)

• •

Using MC, cast on 28 (28, 32, 32) stitches.

Row 1 (RS): K3, *p2, k2, repeat from * to last 0 (0, 0, 1) stitches, k1.

Row 2 (WS): P3, *k2, p2, repeat from * to last 0 (0, 0, 1) stitches, p1. Break MC.

Row 3 (RS): Work as for Row 1.

Working in stripe sequence, shape Sleeve as follows:

Work 3 rows in stockinette stitch.

Increase Row (RS): K1, m1, knit to last stitch, m1, k1.
Work 5 rows in stockinette stitch.
Repeat these 6 rows 6 (6, 7, 7) times more, then work increase row once more. 44 (44, 50, 50) stitches.

Continue in stockinette stitch until work measures 7½ (8, 8½, 9)" (19 [20.5, 21.5, 23]cm).

*(**Note:** You might not end on the last row of the stripe pattern.)*
Work 3 rows in MC. Bind off all stitches.

Finishing

• • •

Block all pieces to the measurements shown in the schematic.

Sew shoulder seams, ending each seam 2¼ (2½, 3, 3¼)" (5.5 [6.5, 7.5, 8]cm) in from the side edge. The neck opening should be 6½ (7, 7, 7½)" (16.5 [17.5, 17.5, 19]cm) wide.

Mark the center of the upper edge of one Sleeve. Match this point to the end of one shoulder seam and sew the upper edge of the Sleeve to the edges of the Front and Back.
Sew the Sleeve seam and side seam, lining up the ends of the stripes.
Repeat for the other Sleeve and side.

Weave in all ends.

• • •

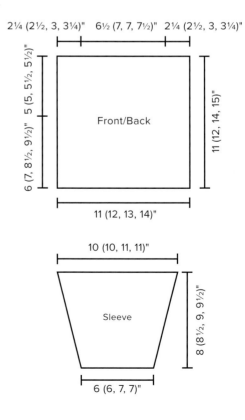

Mimi and Bobbi Beatnik Dolls

What little one wouldn't enjoy the company of these charming beatnik dolls? Bobbi, a fun-loving American, wears a striped sailor dress and styles her hair in twin topknots. Her chic Parisian cousin, Mimi, sports a beret, fuchsia pigtails, and a purple mini. Both dolls are made from the same basic pattern, but their fashionable outfits, hairstyles, and other finishing details give them lots of personality.

DESIGNED BY KAT COYLE

Finished Measurements

• • •

Height: 28" (71cm)

Torso circumference: about 11" (28cm)

Materials

• • •

Brown Sheep Nature Spun Sport Weight, 100% Wool, [184yd (168m) per 50g skein]

BOBBI

[MC] #N03 Grey Heather; 2 skeins

[CC1] #N39 Navy Nite; 1 skein

[CC2] #730 Natural; 1 skein

[CC3] #N17 French Clay; 1 skein

MIMI

[MC] #N94 Bev's Bear; 1 skein

[CC1] #601 Pepper; 1 skein

[CC2] #730 Natural; 1 skein

[CC3] #N62 Amethyst; 1 skein

[CC4] #N46 Red Fox; 1 skein

[CC5] #108 Cherry Delight; 1 skein

Small amounts of yarn are also needed for embroidering the dolls' faces. These are the colors that were used for Mimi and Bobbi:

BOBBI

Mouth: #N46 Red Fox

Eyes: #601 Pepper and #N59 Butterfly Blue

Cheeks: #N87 Victorian Pink

MIMI

Mouth: #N46 Red Fox

Eyes: #601 Pepper and #112 Elf Green

1 set US #5 (3.75mm) straight needles

1 D-3 (3.25mm) crochet hook

Split-ring markers or safety pins

Stitch markers (Mimi only)

Cable needle (Mimi only)

Tapestry needle

Fiberfill stuffing

2" (5cm) pom-pom maker

Gauge

• • •

20 stitches and 30 rows = 4" (10cm) in stockinette stitch

CAFÉ

C6B (Cable 6 Back): Slip the next 3 stitches to the cable needle and hold to the back of the work, k3, k3 from the cable needle.

C6F (Cable 6 Front): Slip the next 3 stitches to the cable needle and hold to the front of the work, k3, k3 from the cable needle.

STRIPE PATTERNS

Bobbi
Right Leg
Cast on using MC.
Work 6 rows using MC. Work 6 rows using CC1.
Repeat these 12 rows until Leg is complete.

Left Leg
Cast on using CC1.
Work 6 rows using CC1. Work 6 rows using MC.
Repeat these 12 rows until Leg is complete.

Dress
Work 6 rows using CC2. Work 2 rows using CC1.
Repeat these 8 rows until Dress is complete.

Mimi
Both Legs
Cast on using CC1.
Work 6 rows using CC1. Work 6 rows using CC2.
Repeat these 12 rows 3 times more, until 48 rows have been worked.
Continue in CC1 only until Leg is complete.

Beret
Work 2 rows using CC1. Work 2 rows using CC2.
Repeat these 4 rows until Beret is complete.

EMBROIDERY STITCHES
Note: If you are not experienced with embroidery on knitted fabric, practice on a swatch before beginning to embroider on your doll. Check suggested reading list and websites on page 142 for resources.

Duplicate Stitch
Duplicate stitch produces the same effect of a knitted-in design by duplicating the path taken by the yarn in a knitted stitch. On the right side of the work, a knit stitch has a "V" shape. Beginning at the base of this V, bring the needle up through the work. At the top right corner of the V, bring the needle back down through the work. Bring the needle behind the work to the upper left corner of the V and draw it up through the work. At the base of the V, bring the needle back down through the work. One duplicate stitch is complete.

Backstitch
Draw the needle up through the work, a short distance from the point where you wish to begin your line of stitching and along the stitching line. At the desired starting point, draw the needle back down through the work. To make the next stitch, bring the needle up through the work, a short distance past the starting point of the previous stitch. Draw the needle back down through the work at the starting point of the previous stitch.
The last stitch in a line of backstitch will begin at the ending point of the stitching line, and will end at the starting point of the previous stitch.

French Knot
Draw the needle upward through the fabric. Holding the yarn taut and flat to the fabric, twist the needle twice around the taut length of yarn, so that the yarn is wrapped twice around the needle. Still holding the yarn taut, insert the needle back into the fabric, very close to the point from which it first emerged. Draw the yarn all the way back through the fabric before releasing the taut length of yarn.

Running Stitch
Weave the needle in and out of the fabric in a straight or curved line, making small, evenly spaced stitches.

• • •

DOLLS

• • •

Legs (Make 2)

• • •

Note: *All the pieces are worked flat and will be sewn later.*

Using the color indicated (see stripe patterns, page 35), cast on 24 stitches.

Working in stripe pattern, work 74 rows in stockinette stitch, ending with a wrong side row.

SHAPE FOOT

• •

Odd-numbered Rows 1–7 (RS): K2, m1, knit to last 2 stitches, m1, k2.

Even-numbered Rows 2–22 (WS): Purl all stitches.

When Row 7 is complete, there are 32 stitches.

Row 9 (RS): K12, k2tog, k4, ssk, k12. 30 stitches.

Row 11 (RS): K2, ssk, k7, k2tog, k4, ssk, k7, k2tog, k2. 26 stitches.

Row 13 (RS): Knit all stitches.

Row 15 (RS): K9, k2tog, k4, ssk, k9. 24 stitches.

Row 17 (RS): Knit all stitches.

Row 19 (RS): K8, k2tog, k4, ssk, k8. 22 stitches.

Row 21 (RS): K7, k2tog, k4, ssk, k7. 20 stitches.

Row 23 (RS): K2, (k2tog) 8 times, k2. 12 stitches.

Row 24 (WS): Purl all stitches. Bind off all stitches.

Torso and Head (Make 2)

• • •

Using MC, cast on 28 stitches.

Work 60 rows in stockinette stitch, ending with a wrong side row.

Place a safety pin or split-ring marker at each end of the last row worked to indicate Arm placement.

SHAPE NECK

• •

Row 1 (RS): K2, ssk, k2, ssk, k12, k2tog, k2, k2tog, k2. 24 stitches.

Rows 2 and 4 (WS): Purl all stitches.

Row 3 (RS): K2, (ssk) 5 times, (k2tog) 5 times, k2. 14 stitches.

Row 5 (RS): K2, (ssk) twice, k2, (k2tog) twice, k2. 10 stitches.

Work 5 rows in stockinette stitch.

SHAPE HEAD

• •

Increase Row (RS): K1, m1, knit to last stitch, m1, k1.

Purl 1 row.

Repeat these two rows 7 times more. 26 stitches.

Work 14 rows in stockinette stitch.

Decrease Row (RS): K2, ssk, knit to last 4 stitches, k2tog, k2.

Purl 1 row.

Repeat these 2 rows 4 times more. 16 stitches.

Next Row (RS): (K2tog) 8 times. 8 stitches.

Purl 1 row. Bind off all stitches.

Arms (Make 2)

• • •

Using MC, cast on 12 stitches.

Work 68 rows in stockinette stitch, ending with a wrong side row.

SHAPE HAND

• •

Increase Row (RS): K1, m1, knit to last stitch, m1, k1.

Purl 1 row.

Repeat these 2 rows once more. 16 stitches.

Work 2 rows in stockinette stitch.

Decrease Row (RS): K1, ssk, knit to last 3 stitches, k2tog, k1.

Purl 1 row.

Repeat these 2 rows 4 times more.

Bind off remaining 6 stitches.

Striped Sailor Mini Dress *(Bobbi)*
• • •

DRESS/BODY (MAKE 2)
• •

Using CC1, cast on 35 stitches.
Knit 2 rows.

Working in stripe pattern, work 34 rows in stockinette stitch, ending with a wrong side row.

Waist Decrease Row (RS): K1, ssk, knit to last 2 stitches, k2tog, k1.
Purl 1 row.
Repeat these 2 rows once more. 31 stitches.
Work 2 rows in stockinette stitch.

Waist Increase Row (RS): K1, m1, knit to last stitch, m1, k1.
Purl 1 row.
Repeat these 2 rows once more. 35 stitches.
Work 22 rows in stockinette stitch.
To form armholes, bind off 4 stitches at the beginning of the next 2 rows. 27 stitches.

Work 12 rows in stockinette stitch.
Bind off all stitches using CC1.

SLEEVES (MAKE 2)
• •

Using CC1, cast on 18 stitches.
Knit 2 rows.

Working in stripe pattern, work 42 rows in stockinette stitch, ending with a wrong side row.

Bind off 4 stitches at the beginning of the next 2 rows. 10 stitches.
Work 12 rows in stockinette stitch. Bind off all stitches using CC1.

Cabled Mini Dress *(Mimi)*
• • •

DRESS/BODY (MAKE 2)
• •

Using CC3, cast on 43 stitches.
Knit 2 rows.

Set-Up Row (RS): K15, place marker, work Row 1 of braid cable chart, place marker, k15.
Continue in pattern as set, working stitches between markers in the charted cable pattern and all other stitches in stockinette stitch, until Dress is complete.

Work 31 rows, ending with a wrong side row.

Waist Decrease Row (RS): K1, ssk, work in pattern to last 2 stitches, k2tog, k1.
Work 1 row.
Repeat these 2 rows once more. 39 stitches.

BRAID CABLE CHART

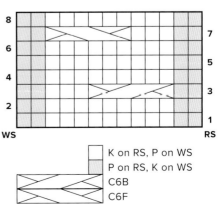

	K on RS, P on WS
	P on RS, K on WS
	C6B
	C6F

Work 2 rows.

Waist Increase Row (RS): K1, m1, work in pattern to last stitch, m1, k1.
Work 1 row.
Repeat these 2 rows once more. 43 stitches.

Work 22 rows.

To form armholes, bind off 4 stitches at the beginning of the next 2 rows. 35 stitches.

Work 12 rows.

Knit 2 rows, removing markers.
Bind off all stitches.

Beret *(Mimi)*
• • •

Using CC1, cast on 60 stitches. Work as follows, working in stripe pattern (see stripe pattern for Beret, in stitch story, page 35).
Row 1 (RS): *K2, p2, repeat from * to end.
Repeat this row 5 times more.

Next Row (RS): *K2, m1, repeat from * to last 2 stitches, k2. 89 stitches.
Work 15 rows in stockinette stitch, ending with a wrong side row.

SHAPE CROWN
• •

Row 1 (RS): *K6, k2tog, repeat from * to last stitch, k1. 78 stitches.
Rows 2–8: Work in stockinette stitch.
Row 9 (RS): *K5, k2tog, repeat from * to last stitch, k1. 67 stitches.
Rows 10–12: Work in stockinette stitch.
Row 13 (RS): *K4, k2tog, repeat from * to last stitch, k1. 56 stitches.
Even-Numbered Rows 14–22 (WS): Purl all stitches.
Row 15 (RS): *K3, k2tog, repeat from * to last stitch, k1. 45 stitches.
Row 17 (RS): *K2, k2tog, repeat from * to last stitch, k1. 34 stitches.

Row 19 (RS): *K1, k2tog, repeat from * to last stitch, k1. 23 stitches.
Row 21 (RS): (K2tog) 11 times, k1. 12 stitches.
Row 23 (RS): (K2tog) 6 times. Cut the yarn, leaving a 12" (30.5cm) tail. Draw this tail through the remaining 6 stitches and pull tight.

Finishing
• • •

Immerse all pieces in lukewarm water and allow them to soak until they are thoroughly saturated. Gently squeeze out water (do not wring!) and lay them on top of several towels on a flat surface. Carefully pin the edges to help flatten the curling edges. Allow them to dry completely.

MOUTH CHART

						5
						4
						3
						2
						1

☐ K on RS, P on WS
▨ P on RS, K on WS

FACES
• •

With red yarn, work the mouth in duplicate stitch, using the mouth chart as a guide.
With black yarn, work the upper outline of each eye using backstitch. Work 5 French knots above each eye, to form eyelashes. Work 1 French knot for the pupil of the eye.

Form the iris of each eye by working blanket stitch in the desired eye color, around each pupil. To work blanket stitch in this way, draw the needle up through the work near the outer edge of the iris, *pass the needle down through the work near the edge of the pupil, then draw the needle up through the work next to the beginning of the previous stitch, catching the strand of the previous stitch with the needle. Repeat from *, working the stitches in a radiating pattern around the pupil until a complete circle has been formed.

Use black yarn and running stitch to form the lower outline of each eye. If eyebrows are desired, work these in running stitching in the yarn used for the hair.

To add detail to cheeks, work 1 stitch in duplicate stitch on each cheek using pink yarn.

DOLL ASSEMBLY
• •

Sew each Leg and Arm together along its long edges, stuffing each piece as you sew it up, and leaving the top ¼" (6mm) unstuffed.

Sew Dress/Body pieces together, beginning near the top of the Head and stuffing as you go. While you are sewing the Body pieces together, insert the tops of the Arms and Legs into the seams at the appropriate points, sewing through all layers to attach the limbs to the torso. The tops of the Arms should be attached just below the marked row at each side of the Dress/Body below the neck; one Leg should be attached at each side of the lower edge of the body, approximately 1" (2.5cm) apart. Leave 1" (2.5cm) open at the top of the Head, to enable you to adjust the stuffing and hair.

For Mimi only, use CC2 to sew boot laces on the CC1 sections of the lower Legs (see photo, page 33).

HAIR
• •

Bobbi
Using CC3 and pom-pom maker, make 2 pom-poms. Sew 1 to each side of the top of the Head, using the photo as a guide.
Cut 170 lengths of CC3, each 28" (71cm) long. Divide these strands into groups of 5. Thread each group of strands through the tapestry needle and sew them to the back of the Head, on either side of the center back, forming a part. The strands should be drawn through the fabric of the Head so that the center of each length of yarn is inside the Head, with the ends on the outside of the Head.

Arrange the hair around the pom-poms and style it into 2 braids. Sew the braids into place on either side of the doll's face. Tie bows at the ends of the braids using CC1. Add more stuffing to the top of the Head, if needed. Sew the Head closed.

Mimi
Cut 85 lengths each of CC4 and CC5 11" (28cm) long. Divide these strands into groups of 3. Thread each group of strands through the tapestry needle and sew them to the back of the Head, knotting them on the inside of the Head. On the Doll shown, the lower layers of hair are CC4, and the upper layers are CC5. Sew strands of both colors above the eyes to form bangs, and trim to the desired length. Style the hair into pigtails and tie with CC3.
Add more stuffing to the top of the Head, if needed.
Sew the Head closed.
Sew the seam of the Beret.
Place the Beret on the Doll's Head and sew it in place.

DRESSES
• •

Striped Dress
Sew Dress/Body pieces together from lower edges to underarms.
Sew the Sleeve seams. Sew the Sleeves to the Dress/Body at underarms, then sew the vertical edges of the sleeve caps to the vertical edges of the armholes. The upper edges of the sleeve caps form part of the neckline of the dress.
Using CC1, work 1 row of single crochet around the neckline of the Dress.
Weave in all ends.

Cabled Dress
Sew Dress/Body pieces together from lower edges to underarms.
Sew shoulder seams, ending each seam approximately 1" (2.5cm) from the armhole edge.
Using CC3, work 1 row of single crochet around the neckline of the Dress.
Weave in all ends.

• • •

TODAY'S BEST SELLERS

Story-time Socks and Footies

Woodland Fairy Wings

Poet Coat

Bite This Book!

Big Idea Vest

At the Bookstore

Books encourage big ideas to take root and the imagination to roam free. So why not knit up some creative items for kids that take their cue from picture books, fairy tales, and poetry? Here are patterns for every little reader, including Woodland Fairy Wings and a thoroughly biteable knitted book. Storytelling is a favorite of the sandbox salon set, and reading is always cool, so this bookstore is the place to be!

Story-time Socks and Footies

What could be cozier than curling up in comfy hand-knit socks while you read a favorite story? These footies and knee socks are worked from the toe up and use short row shaping for the toes and heels. The slipstitch flower pattern along the leg requires patience and produces a tighter gauge than the stockinette stitch.

DESIGNED BY JULIA TRICE

Finished Sizes and Measurements

• • •

FOOTIES

6–12 months (1–2 years, 2–3 years)
Shown in size 6–12 months

Foot circumference: 3¾ (4¼, 4¾)" (9.5 [11, 12]cm)

Foot length: 4¾ (5, 5¼)" (12 [12.5, 13.3]cm)

TALL SOCKS

3 years (4 years)
Shown in size 3 years

Foot circumference: 5¼ (6)" (13.3 [15]cm)

Foot length: 5¾ (6¾)" (14.5 [17]cm)

Leg circumference: 6¼ (7)" (15.8 [18]cm)

When directions are given for both footies and tall socks at the same time, they are given as follows: 6–12 months (1–2 years, 2–3 years, 3 years, 4 years)

Note: Leg and foot sizes can vary significantly from child to child. For best results, measure the length and circumference of the child's foot (around the ball of the foot) to determine which size will best fit the intended recipient. If in doubt, knit a larger size; the child will certainly grow into it!

Materials

• • •

1 (1, 1, 2, 2) skeins Louet Gems, 100% Superwash Merino Wool [185yd (169m) per 50g skein]
Color: Willow

Note: 2 skeins will make a pair of tall socks and at least one pair of footies.

1 set US #1 (2.25mm) double-pointed needles

Note: If the recipient of the socks has calves with a circumference of more than 9 (10)" (23 [25.5]cm), you may wish to work the legs of the tall socks using US #2 (2.75mm) needles.

1 US C/2 (2.75mm) crochet hook

Smooth waste yarn

Safety pin or split-ring marker

Yarn needle

Gauge

• • •

32 stitches = 4" (10cm) in stockinette stitch

CROCHET CAST-ON

Using waste yarn, work a crochet chain several stitches longer than the number of stitches to be cast on. Starting 1 or 2 stitches in from the end of the chain and using the working yarn, pick up and knit 1 stitch in the back loop of each chain stitch until the required number of stitches have been worked. Later, the chain will be unraveled and the resulting live stitches picked up.

WRAP AND TURN

Note: Used when working short rows.
To wrap and turn on a RS row, knit to point specified in pattern, bring yarn to front of work between needles, slip next stitch to right-hand needle, bring yarn around this stitch to back of work, slip stitch back to left-hand needle, turn work to begin purling back in the other direction.

To wrap and turn on a WS row, purl to point specified in pattern, bring yarn to back of work between needles, slip next stitch to right-hand needle, bring yarn around this stitch to front of work, slip stitch back to left-hand needle, turn work to begin knitting back in the other direction.

WORKING WRAPS TOGETHER
WITH WRAPPED STITCHES:

When you encounter a wrapped stitch, work the wrap together with the wrapped stitch as follows:

When working a RS row, knit to wrapped stitch. Slip next stitch from left needle to right needle, use the tip of the left needle to pick up the wrap and place it on right needle, insert left needle into both wrap and stitch, and knit them together.

When working a WS row, purl to wrapped stitch. Slip the next stitch from left needle to right needle, use the tip of the left needle to pick up the wrap and place it on the right needle, slip both wrap and stitch back to left needle, purl together through back loops.

• • •

FOOTIES AND TALL SOCKS
• • •
Toe
• • •

Using the crochet cast-on method, cast on 15 (17, 19, 21, 24) stitches.
Row 1 (WS): Purl all stitches.
Row 2 (RS): K14 (16, 18, 20, 23), wrap and turn.
Row 3 (WS): P13 (15, 17, 19, 22), wrap and turn.
Continue working short rows in this way, working each row 1 stitch shorter than the last, until:
Row 13 (15, 17, 17, 19) (WS): P3 (3, 3, 5, 6), wrap and turn.

While working the short rows that follow, when you come to a wrapped stitch, pick up the wrap and work it together with the stitch it wraps.

When wrapping stitches at the turning points of the short rows that follow, note that stitches will now have two wraps. When working a double-wrapped stitch on a subsequent row, pick up both wraps and work them together with the wrapped stitch.

Next Row (RS): K4 (4, 4, 6, 7), wrap and turn.
Next Row (WS): P5 (5, 5, 7, 8), wrap and turn.
Continue working short rows in this way, working each row 1 stitch longer than the last, until:
Last Row (RS): K14 (16, 18, 20, 23). Do not turn. 1 stitch remains wrapped at the beginning of this row; work the wraps on this stitch together with the stitch when working the first round of the Foot.

Foot

• • •

Remove the crochet chain from the cast-on edge and divide the resulting 15 (17, 19, 21, 24) live stitches between two needles, placing 8 (9, 10, 11, 12) stitches on the first needle and 7 (8, 9, 10, 12) stitches on the second needle. Knit across these stitches. You will be at the point between the last stitch from the cast-on edge and the last wrapped stitch of the short-row toe. This point is now the beginning of the round. If desired, place a safety pin or split-ring marker in your work to indicate the beginning of the round.

The first, second, and third needles in the round will be designated needle 1, needle 2, and needle 3, respectively. There are 30 (34, 38, 42, 48) stitches in total, divided as follows:
Needle 1: 15 (17, 19, 21, 24) stitches
Needle 2: 8 (9, 10, 11, 12) stitches
Needle 3: 7 (8, 9, 10, 12) stitches

FOOTIES ONLY

• •

Knit 3 (3, 4) rounds.

Begin Flower Pattern
Round 1: K7 (8, 9), (k1, yo, k1, yo, k1) in next stitch, knit to end.
Round 2: K7 (8, 9); k5 wrapping yarn around needle twice when working each stitch, knit to end.

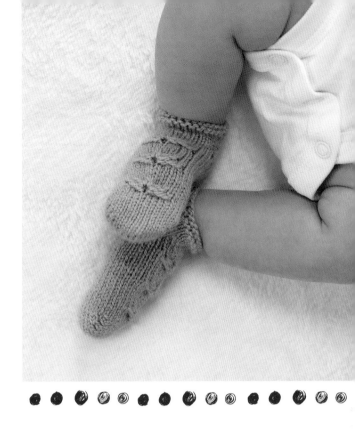

Round 3: K3 (4, 5), slip the next 4 stitches to the right needle, drop the next stitch (an elongated stitch) from the left needle and let it fall to the front of the work, slip the 4 slipped stitches back to the left needle, pick up the dropped stitch and place it on the left needle (it will only be wrapped around the needle once), knit this stitch together with the next stitch through their back loops; k3, slip the next 3 (elongated) stitches to the right needle, dropping the second wrap of each stitch; drop the next stitch (the last elongated stitch) from the left needle and let it fall to the front of the work, k3, slip the next stitch to the right needle, pick up the dropped stitch and place it on the left needle, slip the slipped stitch back to the left needle and knit it together with the elongated stitch; knit to end.

Round 4: K4 (5, 6), slip the next 3 stitches to the right needle, drop the next stitch from the left needle and let it fall to the front of the work, slip the 3 slipped stitches back to the left needle, pick up the dropped stitch and place it on the left needle, knit this stitch together with the next stitch, through their back loops; k2, slip the next stitch to the right needle; drop the next stitch from the left needle and let it fall to the front of the work, k2, slip the next stitch to the right needle, pick up the dropped stitch and place it on the left needle, slip the slipped stitch back to the left needle and knit it together with the elongated stitch; knit to end.

Rounds 5–8 (5–9, 5–9): Knit all stitches.

Repeat Rounds 1–8 (1–9, 1–9) twice more.
Knit 1 (0, 1) round.
Proceed to the Heel.

TALL SOCKS ONLY
• •
Knit all rounds until the work measures 4¼ (5½)" (11 [13.3]cm) from the tip of the toe.
Proceed to the Heel.

Heel
• • •
Work the Heel in the same way as you worked the Toe, working over the stitches on needles 2 and 3 only.

Leg
• • •
FOOTIES ONLY
• •
Knit 5 (5, 7) rounds.
Purl 1 round.
Knit 1 round.
Loosely bind off all stitches purlwise.

Weave in all ends.

TALL SOCKS ONLY
• •
Note: If you plan to use larger needles for the calf, switch to the larger needles after the first 5 rounds have been worked.
Size 3 years only:
Round 1: *K3, m1, k4, m1, repeat from * to end. 54 stitches.
Size 4 years only:
Round 1: *K4, m1, repeat from * to end. 60 stitches.
All sizes:
Divide the stitches evenly between the needles: Each needle has 18 (20) stitches.

Rounds 2–5: Knit all stitches.

Round 6: K13 (15), *(k1, yo, k1, yo, k1) in next stitch, k17 (19), repeat from * once more, (k1, yo, k1, yo, k1) in next stitch, k4.

Round 7: K13 (15), *k5 wrapping yarn around needle twice when working each stitch; k17 (19), repeat from * once more, k5 wrapping yarn around needle twice when working each stitch; k4.

Round 8: *K9 (11), slip the next 4 stitches to the right needle, drop the next stitch (an elongated stitch) from the left needle and let it fall to the front of the work, slip the 4 slipped stitches back to the left needle, pick up the dropped stitch and place it on the left needle (it will only be wrapped around the needle once). Knit this stitch together with the next stitch through their back loops; k3, slip the next 3 (elongated) stitches to the right needle, dropping the second wrap of each stitch; drop the next stitch (the last elongated stitch) from the left needle and let it fall to the front of the work, k3, slip the next stitch to the right needle, pick up the dropped stitch and place it on the left needle, slip the slipped stitch back to the left needle and knit it together with the elongated stitch, repeat from * twice more.

Round 9: *K10 (12), slip the next 3 stitches to the right needle, drop the next stitch from the left needle and let it fall to the front of the work, slip the 3 slipped stitches back to the left needle, pick up the dropped stitch and place it on the left needle, knit this stitch together with the next stitch, through their back loops; k2, slip the next stitch to the right needle; drop the next stitch from the left needle and let it fall to the front of the work, k2, slip the next stitch to the right needle, pick up the dropped stitch and place it on the left needle, slip the slipped stitch back to the left needle and knit it together with the elongated stitch; k1, repeat from * twice more.

Round 10: Knit all stitches.

Round 11: K4 (5), *(k1, yo, k1, yo, k1) in next stitch, k17 (19), repeat from * once more, (k1, yo, k1, yo, k1) in next stitch, k13 (14).

Round 12: K4 (5), *k5 wrapping yarn around needle twice when working each stitch; k17 (19), repeat from * once more, k5 wrapping yarn around needle twice when working each stitch; k13 (14).

Round 13: K0 (1), *slip the next 4 stitches to the right needle, drop the next stitch from the left needle and let it fall to the front of the work, slip the 4 slipped stitches back to the left needle, pick up the dropped stitch and place it on the left needle, knit this stitch together with the next stitch, through their back loops; k3, slip the next 3 stitches to the right needle, dropping the second wrap of each stitch; drop the next stitch from the left needle and let it fall to the front of the work, k3, slip the next stitch to the right needle, pick up the dropped stitch and place it on the left needle, slip the slipped stitch back to the left needle and knit it together with the elongated stitch; k9 (11), repeat from * twice more, ending the last repeat with (k9 [10]) instead of (k9 [11]).

Round 14: K1 (2), *slip the next 3 stitches to the right needle, drop the next stitch from the left needle and let it fall to the front of the work, slip the 3 slipped stitches back to the left needle, pick up the dropped stitch and place it on the left needle, knit this stitch together with the next stitch, through their back loops; k2, slip the next stitch to the right needle; drop the next stitch from the left needle and let it fall to the front of the work, k2, slip the next stitch to the right needle, pick up the dropped stitch and place it on the left needle, slip the slipped stitch back to the left needle and knit it together with the elongated stitch; k11 (13), repeat from * twice more, ending the last repeat with (k10 [11]) instead of (k11 [13]).

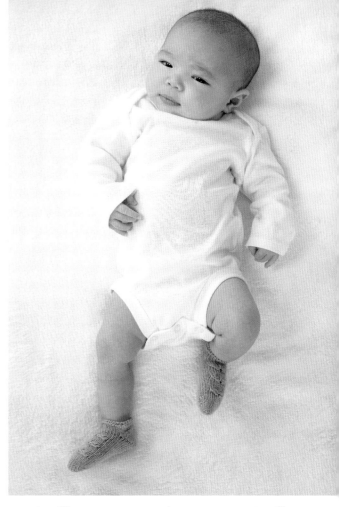

Round 15: Knit all stitches.
Repeat Rounds 6–15 6 (7) times more, then work Rounds 6–10 once more.
15 (17) rows of flowers have been worked.

Knit 3 rounds.

Next Round: *K1, p1, repeat from * to end.
Repeat this round 6 (8) times more.

Next Round: *Kfb, p1, repeat from * to end.

Next Round: *K2, p1, repeat from * to end.
Repeat this round 0(1) time more.
Bind off all stitches in pattern.

Weave in all ends.

• • •

Woodland Fairy Wings

Delight your favorite pixie with these enchanting fairy wings. Knit with kid mohair in lace stitches as delicate as gossamer, the wings are gathered and sewn to the golden crocheted center-piece. Crocheted ties wrap around your little sprite's waist, and her arms slide through wrist loops, so she's ready to practice her flying skills wherever her imagination takes her.

DESIGNED BY KAT COYLE

• • • STITCH STORY • • •

Basic crochet skills are needed for this project. Check suggested reading list and websites on page 142 for resources.

• • •

WINGS (MAKE 2)

• • •

While working Wings, alternate 2 rows MC with 2 rows CC throughout. Carry the yarn not in use along the side edge of the work.

Using MC and the long-tail cast-on method, loosely cast on 83 stitches.
56

Finished Size and Measurements

• • •

To fit 3 years and up

Width from wing tip to wing tip *(between wrist loops):* 33" (84cm)

Length of wing at side edge: 31" (79cm)

Length at center back: 13" (33cm)

Length of long tie: 75" (190.5cm)

Materials

• • •

Crystal Palace Kid Merino, 28% Kid Mohair / 28% Merino Wool / 44% Micro Nylon, [240yd (219m) per 25g ball], 1 ball each MC and CC1

[MC] #9806 Fern Mix

[CC1] #4671 Lime Sherbet

[CC2] Crystal Palace Deco-Stardust, 55% Lurex / 45% Nylon, [119yd (109m) per 50g ball], color: #4437 Gold, 1 ball

1 pair US 10.5 (6.5mm) straight needles [15 handwritten]

1 US H-8 (5mm) crochet hook

Stitch holder

Yarn needle

Gauge

• • •

Approximately 10 stitches and 17 rows = 4" (10cm) in Wing Lace pattern

Note: Exact gauge is not important for this project.

WING LACE CHART

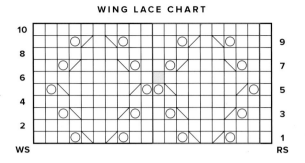

BORDER LACE CHART

K on RS, P on WS
P on RS, K on WS
○ YO
K2

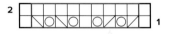

3erows winglace

Wor... ...hart, page 50.
Work 40 r...

Next Row (RS): Work 29 stitches in pattern; place remaining 54 stitches on stitch holder.

Work 8 rows in pattern.
Next Row (WS): Bind off 18 stitches, work in pattern to end. 11 stitches.
Work 10 rows in pattern.
Bind off all stitches using both yarns held together.

Replace the held stitches to the needle with the right side facing and reattach both yarns.

Next Row (RS): Bind off 25 stitches with both yarns held together, work in pattern to end (using 1 yarn).

Work 9 rows in pattern.
Next Row (RS): Bind off 18 stitches using both yarns held together, work in pattern to end.
Work 9 rows in pattern.
Bind off all stitches using both yarns held together.

LONG TIE

Using CC2, chain 301.
Row 1: Work 1 single crochet in second chain from hook and in each chain to end.
Row 2: Chain 1, work 1 single crochet in each stitch to end.
Repeat Row 2 once more. Cut the yarn, draw through last stitch, and pull tight.

CENTER BACK PIECE

Using CC2, chain 49.
Row 1: Work 1 single crochet in second chain from hook and in each chain to end.
Row 2: Chain 1, work 1 single crochet in each stitch to end.
Repeat Row 2 five times more. Cut the yarn, leaving a 12" (30.5cm) tail, draw through last stitch and pull tight. Fold the end of this strip up 2" (5cm) and sew the end in place, forming a loop.

WRIST LOOPS (MAKE 2)

Using CC2, chain 49.
Row 1: Work 1 single crochet in second chain from hook and in each chain to end.
Row 2: Chain 1, work 1 single crochet in each stitch to end.
Repeat Row 2 once more. Cut the yarn, leaving a 12" (30.5cm) tail, draw through last stitch and pull tight.

Finishing

Immerse both Wings in lukewarm water and allow them to soak until they are thoroughly saturated. Gently squeeze out the water (do not wring!) and lay the Wings on top of several towels on a flat surface. Carefully pin the Wings out to the dimensions given. Allow them to dry completely.

GATHER WINGS

Row 1 (RS): Using CC1, with right side facing, work 116 single crochet along the shaped bound-off edge of one Wing; this will be vapproximately 1 stitch in each bound-off stitch and each row edge.

Row 2 (WS): Chain 1, single crochet in first 2 stitches, *skip next stitch, single crochet in next 2 stitches, repeat from * to end. 78 stitches.

Row 3 (RS): Chain 1, skip first stitch, single crochet in next 2 stitches, *skip next stitch, single crochet in next 2 stitches, repeat from * to end. 52 stitches.

Row 4 (WS): Chain 1, single crochet in first stitch, *skip next stitch, single crochet in next 2 stitches, repeat from * to end. 35 stitches.

Row 5 (RS): Chain 1, single crochet in first 2 stitches, *skip next stitch, single crochet in next 2 stitches, repeat from * to end. 24 stitches. Cut the yarn, draw through last stitch and pull tight.

The gathered edge of the Wing will be approximately 9" (23cm) long.

Gather the second Wing in the same way; leave a long tail when cutting the yarn.

Use this tail to sew the Wings together along the short, gathered edges, ensuring that the right sides of both Wings are facing the same way.

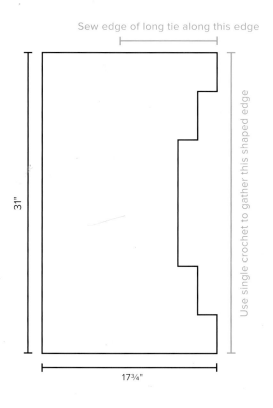

Sew edge of long tie along this edge

Use single crochet to gather this shaped edge

31"

17¾"

ASSEMBLY

• • •

Lay the Wings flat, with their right sides facing up. Lay the Center Back Piece on top of the seam between the Wings, so that the loop protrudes below the bottom of the Wings. Sew this piece to the Wings, sewing first along the center, then along the edges of the piece.

Sew the center of the Long Tie to the top of the Center Back Piece (opposite the loop). Sew the edge of the Long Tie along the top edge of each Wing for 9" (23cm), leaving the rest of each Wing free.

Fold one Wrist Loop in half and sandwich approximately 1½" (3.8cm) of the upper corner of one Wing between the ends of the Loop. Sew the Loop ends and Wing tip firmly together. Sew the other Wrist Loop to the other Wing in the same way.

To wear, place the Wings behind the wearer's back with the Long Tie at their shoulders. Drape the Long Tie over the shoulders, cross it in front of the chest, wrap it behind the back and thread both ends through the loop at the base of the Center Back Piece. Bring the ends around to the front of the waist and tie them. The wearer can then slip their hands through the Wrist Loops and take flight!

• • •

Poet Coat

With its sweeping tail and distinguished collar and cuffs, this dashing coat is just right for the gentle poet of the house and a splendid project for the more advanced knitter. The fabric is worked in linen stitch, which adds body without increasing bulkiness. A practical zipper closure is trimmed with gold stars, as are the collar and cuffs. The final flourish—an orange I-cord trim—unifies the design with flair.

DESIGNED BY MARNIE MACLEAN

Finished Sizes and Measurements

• • •

6–12 months (1–2 years, 2–3 years, 3–4 years)
Shown in size 3–4 years

Chest: 22 (25½, 26, 27)" (56 [64.8, 66, 68.6]cm)

Length: 16 (18, 20, 22)" (40.5 [45.5, 51, 56]cm)

Materials

• • •

Blue Sky Alpaca Melange, 100% Baby Alpaca, [110yd (100m) per 50g skein]

[MC] #800 Cornflower; 8 (9, 9, 9) skeins

[CC] #801 Orange Zest; 2 skeins

1 set US #2 (2.75mm) double-pointed needles

1 set US #6 (4mm) double-pointed needles

1 US #6 (4mm) circular needle, 24" (60cm) or longer

1 US #2 (2.75mm) circular needle, any length (optional)

Yarn needle

Ten ¾" (20mm) gold star buttons (shown) OR star-shaped appliqués for smaller children

Six ⅝" (16mm) gold star buttons (shown) OR star-shaped appliqués for smaller children

Embroidery thread to match both shades of yarn (used for sewing buttons and zipper)

Sewing needle

12" (30.5cm) separating zipper in coordinating color

Gauge

• • •

29.5 stitches and 50 rows = 4" (10 cm) in linen stitch using US #6 (4mm) needles

24 stitches and 36 rows = 4" (10cm) in stockinette stitch using US #2 (2.75mm) needles

••• STITCH STORY •••

LINEN STITCH (FOR COAT BODY)
Note: Worked back and forth over an even number of stitches.

Row 1 (RS): *K1, sl 1 with yarn held to front of work, repeat from * to last 2 stitches, k2.
Row 2 (WS): *P1, sl 1 with yarn held to back of work, repeat from * to last 2 stitches, p2.
Repeat these 2 rows for linen stitch.

LINEN STITCH (FOR COAT SLEEVES)
Note: Worked in the round over an even number of stitches.

Round 1: *K1, sl 1 with yarn held to front of work, repeat from * to last 2 stitches, k2.
Round 2: K2, *sl 1 with yarn held to front of work, k1, repeat from * to end.
Repeat these 2 rounds for linen stitch.

SEED STITCH
Note: Worked over an odd number of stitches.

Row 1: *K1, p1, repeat from * to last stitch, k1.
Repeat this row for seed stitch.

WRAP AND TURN
Note: Used when working short rows.

To wrap and turn on a RS row, work to point specified in pattern, bring yarn to front of work between needles, slip next stitch to right-hand needle, bring yarn around this stitch to back of work, slip stitch back to left-hand needle, turn work to begin working back in the other direction.

To wrap and turn on a WS row, work to point specified in pattern, bring yarn to back of work between needles, slip next stitch to right-hand needle, bring yarn around this stitch to front of work, slip stitch back to left-hand needle, turn work to begin working back in the other direction.

THREE-NEEDLE BIND-OFF
Hold both pieces of knitting with right sides together. Insert needle into the first stitch on the front needle and first stitch on the back needle, and knit them together.
Repeat this for the next stitch on the front and back needles. Draw the first stitch worked over the second stitch.
Repeat from * to * until all stitches have been bound off. Cut the yarn and draw it through the remaining stitch.

• • •

COAT
• • •

LOWER BODY
• •

Using the US #6 (4mm) circular needle and MC, cast on 144 (154, 156, 162) stitches. Place a stitch marker 25 (25, 25, 26) stitches from each end; there will be 94 (104, 106, 110) stitches between the markers. These markers indicate the placement of the side "seams."

The body of the Coat is worked entirely in linen stitch back and forth in rows. When working the short rows that follow, it is not necessary to work wraps together with wrapped stitches (as you would when working short rows in stockinette stitch). The texture of the linen stitch fabric will hide the short row wraps.

Shape Lower Edge
Row 1 (RS): Work 83 (88, 89, 92) stitches in pattern, wrap and turn.
Row 2 (WS): Work 22 stitches in pattern, wrap and turn.
Row 3 (RS): Work 27 stitches in pattern, wrap and turn.
Row 4 (WS): Work 32 stitches in pattern, wrap and turn.
Row 5 (RS): Work 35 stitches in pattern, wrap and turn.
Row 6 (WS): Work 38 stitches in pattern, wrap and turn.
Row 7 (RS): Work 41 stitches in pattern, wrap and turn.
Row 8 (WS): Work 44 stitches in pattern, wrap and turn.
Row 9 (RS): Work 48 stitches in pattern, wrap and turn.
Row 10 (WS): Work 52 stitches in pattern, wrap and turn.
Row 11 (RS): Work to end of row.

Important: Read ahead. The sections titled "Shape Front Edges," below, and "Shape Sides," page 56, are worked at the same time, beginning on the next row, which is a wrong side row.

Shape Front Edges

The increase rows that shape the front edges of this coat are worked on both right side and wrong side rows. The Increase Row is worked as follows:

Increase Row (RS or WS): Work 1 stitch, m1, work in pattern to last stitch, m1, work last stitch.

The front edge shaping is worked differently for each size.

Size 6–12 months only:
Work 2 Increase Rows.
Work 1 row in pattern.
Repeat these 3 rows 5 times more.

Work Increase Row.
Work 1 row in pattern.
Repeat these 2 rows 3 times more.

Work Increase Row.
Work 3 rows in pattern.
Repeat these 4 rows 3 times more.

Work Increase Row.
Work 6 rows in pattern.
Work Increase Row once more.
22 Increase Rows have been worked.

Size 1–2 years only:
Work 3 Increase Rows.
Work 1 row in pattern.
Repeat these 4 rows 3 times more.

Work Increase Row.
Work 1 row in pattern.
Repeat these 2 rows 4 times more.

Work Increase Row.
Work 2 rows in pattern.
Repeat these 3 rows 3 times more.

Work Increase Row.
Work 3 rows in pattern.
Repeat these 4 rows once more.

Work Increase Row.
Work 4 rows in pattern.
Work Increase Row.
Work 7 rows in pattern.
Work Increase Row.
26 Increase Rows have been worked.

Size 2–3 years only:

Work 3 Increase Rows.

Work 1 row in pattern.

Repeat these 4 rows 3 times more.

Work Increase Row.

Work 1 row in pattern.

Repeat these 2 rows 4 times more.

Work Increase Row.

Work 2 rows in pattern.

Repeat these 3 rows 7 times more.

Work Increase Row.

Work 4 rows in pattern.

Repeat these 5 rows once more.

Work Increase Row.

Work 8 rows in pattern.

Work Increase Row.

29 Increase Rows have been worked.

Size 3–4 years only:

Work 3 Increase Rows.

Work 1 row in pattern.

Repeat these 4 rows twice more.

Work Increase Row.

Work 1 row in pattern.

Repeat these 2 rows 5 times more.

Work Increase Row.

Work 2 rows in pattern.

Repeat these 3 rows 6 times more.

Work Increase Row.

Work 3 rows in pattern.

Repeat these 4 rows twice more.

Work Increase Row.

Work 5 rows in pattern.

Repeat these 6 rows once more.

Work Increase Row.

Work 9 rows in pattern.

Work Increase Row.

29 Increase Rows have been worked.

All Sizes:

22 (26, 29, 29) Increase Rows have been worked. Including short rows, a total of 61 (71, 81, 91) rows have been worked. Measured at center back, the work is approximately 5 (5¾, 6½, 7¼)" (12.5 [14.5, 16.5, 18.5]cm) long.

At the same time, the Lower Body is shaped at the side "seams" as follows:

Shape Sides

Work 1 (5, 7, 9) rows in linen stitch.

Decrease Row (RS): Work in pattern to 2 stitches before first marker, k2tog, ssk, work in pattern to 2 stitches before second marker, k2tog, ssk, work in pattern to end.

Work 23 (31, 35, 39) rows in pattern.

Repeat these 24 (32, 36, 40) rows 4 (3, 3, 3) times more.

Work Decrease Row once more.

When all front edge and side shaping has been completed, there will be 164 (186, 194, 200) stitches. Each Front has 41 (46, 49, 50) stitches, and the Back has 82 (94, 96, 100) stitches.

Work 7 (13, 17, 21) rows in pattern. You will have just completed a wrong side row.
Including short rows, 139 (157, 179, 201) rows have been worked. Measured at center back, the work is 11 (12½, 14¼, 16)" (28 [32, 36, 40.5]cm) long.

Divide for Armholes
Next Row (RS): Work in pattern to 4 (5, 6, 6) stitches before first marker, bind off next 8 (10, 12, 12) stitches, place the 37 (41, 43, 44) stitches just worked on a stitch holder; work in pattern to 4 (5, 6, 6) stitches before second marker, bind off next 8 (10, 12, 12) stitches, place the 74 (84, 84, 88) stitches just worked on a stitch holder, work in pattern to end. 37 (41, 43, 44) stitches.

LEFT FRONT
• •
Work 1 row in pattern.
Next Row (RS): K1, ssk, work in pattern to end.
Repeat these 2 rows 3 (5, 5, 5) times more. 33 (35, 37, 38) stitches.

Work 28 (30, 32, 36) rows in pattern.

Shape Neckline
Row 1 (WS): Bind off 6 (7, 7, 7) stitches, work in pattern to end. 27 (28, 30, 31) stitches.

Row 2 (RS): Work in pattern to last 3 stitches, k2tog, k1.
Row 3 (WS): P1, p2tog, work in pattern to end.
Repeat Rows 2 and 3 twice more, then work Row 2, 1 (0, 1, 1) time more. 20 (22, 23, 24) stitches.

Work 16 (18, 18, 18) rows in pattern.
Cut the yarn and place all stitches on a stitch holder.

RIGHT FRONT
• •
Replace the held stitches of the Right Front on the needle with the wrong side facing, and reattach the yarn.

Work 1 row in pattern.
Next Row (RS): Work in pattern to last 3 stitches, k2tog, k1.
Repeat these 2 rows 3 (5, 5, 5) times more. 33 (35, 37, 38) stitches.

Work 27 (29, 31, 35) rows in pattern.

Shape Neckline
Row 1 (RS): Bind off 6 (7, 7, 7) stitches, work in pattern to end. 27 (28, 30, 31) stitches.

Row 2 (WS): Work in pattern to last 3 stitches, p2tog tbl, p1.
Row 3 (RS): K1, ssk, work in pattern to end.
Repeat Rows 2 and 3 twice more, then work Row 2, 1 (0, 1, 1) time more. 20 (22, 23, 24) stitches.

Work 17 (19, 19, 19) rows in pattern.
Cut the yarn and place all stitches on a stitch holder.

BACK
• •
Replace the held stitches of the Back on the needle with the wrong side facing and reattach the yarn.

Work 1 row in pattern.
Next Row (RS): K1, ssk, work in pattern to last 3 stitches, k2tog, k1.
Repeat these 2 rows 3 (5, 5, 5) times more. 66 (72, 72, 76) stitches.

Work 48 (50, 53, 57) rows in pattern.

Shape Neckline
Next Row: Work 20 (22, 23, 24) stitches in pattern, join a new ball of yarn and bind off 26 (28, 26, 28) stitches, work the remaining 20 (22, 23, 24) stitches in pattern.

Working both of the sets of stitches on the needle with separate balls of yarn, work 3 (4, 4, 4) rows in pattern.

Including short rows, 199 (224, 249, 275) rows have been worked. Measured along center back from lower edge to top of shoulder, the work is approximately 16 (18, 20, 22)" (40.5 [45.5, 51, 56]cm) long.

Join Shoulders

Place the held stitches of one Front shoulder on a double-pointed needle, and join it to the corresponding Back shoulder using a three-needle bind-off. Join the other shoulder in the same way.

SLEEVES

• •

Using US #6 (4mm) double-pointed needles and MC, with right side facing and beginning at center of bound-off stitches of left underarm, pick up and knit 1 stitch in each bound-off stitch to shaped front armhole edge. Pick up and knit 26 (28, 28, 29) stitches along front armhole edge and 26 (28, 28, 29) stitches along back armhole edge (approximately 2 stitches for every 5 rows), pick up and knit 1 stitch in each remaining bound-off stitch at underarm. 60 (66, 68, 70) stitches. Place a marker to indicate the beginning of the round.

The Sleeves are worked in linen stitch. The sleeve caps are worked flat using short rows, then the Sleeves are worked in the round down to the wrist.

Shape Sleeve Cap

Row 1 (RS): Work 34 (37, 38, 39) stitches in pattern, wrap and turn.
Row 2 (WS): Work 8 stitches in pattern, wrap and turn.
Row 3 (RS): Work 9 stitches in pattern, wrap and turn.
Row 4 (WS): Work 10 stitches in pattern, wrap and turn.

Continue in this way, working each short row 1 stitch longer than the last, until:

Row 46 (50, 50, 52) (WS): Work 52 (56, 56, 58) stitches in pattern, wrap and turn.
Next Row (RS): Work in pattern to end of round. The sleeve cap is complete.

Shape Sleeve

Work 3 (3, 7, 7) rounds in pattern.

Decrease Round: K2tog, work in pattern to last 2 stitches, ssk.
Work 8 (9, 11, 13) rounds in pattern.
Repeat these 9 (10, 12, 14) rounds 6 (8, 6, 6) times more, then work Decrease Round once more. 44 (46, 52, 52, 54) stitches.

Work 4 (4, 8, 8) rounds in pattern. Cut MC.
From the underarm, 72 (99, 101, 115) rounds have been worked. Measured from underarm to lower edge, the sleeve is 5¾ (8, 8, 9¼)" (14.5 [20.5, 20.5, 23.5]cm) long.

Cuff

The cuff is worked using CC and US #2 (2.75mm) double-pointed needles, in stockinette stitch and seed stitch.

The beginning of the row for the cuff is at a different point from the beginning of the round for the sleeve. The new starting point will be 11 (12, 13, 14) stitches from the previous end of the round, toward the back of the Sleeve.

Turn the Coat inside out. Rearrange the stitches on the needles so that you can begin a new row at this point. To be sure you are at the correct point, lay the Coat flat, with the Back facing up. The new starting point should be at the center of the edge of the Sleeve that is facing you.

The cuff will be worked with its right side facing, though the wrong side of the Sleeve is facing. This is so that when the cuff is folded back its right side will be facing.

Attach CC at the new starting point, with the wrong side of the Sleeve facing, and work as follows using US #2 (2.75mm) double-pointed needles:

Round 1: *K2, k2tog, repeat from * to last 0 (2, 0, 2) stitches, k0 (2, 0, 2). 33 (35, 39, 41) stitches.

Knit 10 (10, 12, 12) rounds.

Turn work so that the wrong side of the cuff is facing. From this point, the cuff will be worked back and forth in rows.

Row 1 (WS): Knit all stitches.
Row 2 (RS): Work 5 stitches in seed stitch, m1, knit to last 5 stitches, m1, work in seed stitch to end.
Row 3 (WS): Work 5 stitches in seed stitch, purl to last 5 stitches, work in seed stitch to end.
Repeat Rows 2 and 3, 5 (5, 6, 6) times more, then work Row 2 once more. 47 (49, 55, 57) stitches.
Work 1 row in seed stitch.
Next Row (RS): Work 5 stitches in seed stitch, m1, work in seed stitch to last 5 stitches, m1, work in seed stitch to end.
Repeat these 2 rows twice more, then work 1 more wrong side row. 53 (55, 61, 63) stitches.
Bind off all stitches in pattern.

Work the Right Sleeve and cuff in the same way.

COLLAR

. .

Turn Coat right side out.

With wrong side facing, using CC and US #2 (2.75mm) circular or double-pointed needle(s), beginning at the point where the decreases begin on the left front neckline edge (*after* the bound off neckline stitches), pick up and knit stitches as follows:
18 (19, 20, 22) stitches along the shaped left vertical neckline edge, placing a marker at the shoulder seam;

26 (27, 27, 29) stitches along the back neckline edge; 18 (19, 20, 22) stitches along the shaped right vertical neckline edge, placing a marker at the shoulder seam. 62 (65, 67, 73) stitches.
As with the cuffs, the right side of the collar will be worked with the wrong side of the jacket facing.

Next Row (RS): *K2, k2tog, repeat from * to last 2 (1, 3, 1) stitches, k2 (1, 3, 1). 47 (49, 51, 55) stitches.
Work 1 row in seed stitch.

Shape Collar
Continue in seed stitch as follows, working new stitches into pattern:
Row 1 (RS): K1, m1, work in pattern to last stitch, m1, k1.
Row 2 (WS): Work in pattern.
Row 3 (RS): K1, m1, work in pattern to marker, m1, slip marker, work 1 stitch, m1, work in pattern to 1 stitch before marker, m1, work 1 stitch, slip marker, m1, work in pattern to last stitch, m1, k1.
Row 4 (WS): Work in pattern.
Repeat these 4 rows 2 (2, 3, 3) times more, then for first two sizes only work rows 1 and 2 once more. 73 (75, 83, 87) stitches.

Next Row: K2tog, work in pattern to last 2 stitches, k2tog.
Repeat this row 5 times more.
Bind off remaining 61 (63, 71, 75) stitches.

Edging

Beginning at the Right Front neckline edge next to the Collar, work applied I-Cord along the Right Front neckline edge, down the Right Front edge, along the lower Back edge, up the Left Front edge, and along the Left Front neckline edge to the edge of the Collar, as follows:

Using US #2 (2.75mm) double-pointed needles and CC, cast on 2 stitches.
Slide the stitches to the end of the needle, so that the stitch that is not connected to the working yarn is ready to be worked.
*Bring the yarn around the back of the work, knit the first stitch on the needle, insert the tip of the left needle into the edge of the fabric and pick up a stitch, knit this stitch together with the second stitch on the needle. Slide the stitches to the other end of the needle and transfer this needle back to your left hand.
Repeat from * until applied I-Cord is complete.
Bind off both stitches. Use the yarn tails at each end of the I-Cord to sew the ends of the I-Cord to the edges of the Collar.

Finishing

• • •

Weave in all ends.
Immerse the Coat in lukewarm water and allow it to soak until it is thoroughly saturated. Gently squeeze out the water (do not wring!) and lay the Coat on top of several towels on a flat surface. Carefully pin the Coat out to the dimensions given, with the collar folded down and the cuffs folded back. Allow it to dry completely.

Sew the zipper inside the front edges of the Coat, with the bottom of the zipper aligned to the last front edge increase row.

Using the photos as guides, sew the larger star-shaped buttons or appliqués to the front edges of the Coat.

Sew four small buttons or appliqués to the cuffs, using them as cufflinks, to hold the two halves of each cuff together. Sew the remaining two small buttons or appliqués to the collar, sewing through both the collar and the Coat body to tack the collar down.

• • •

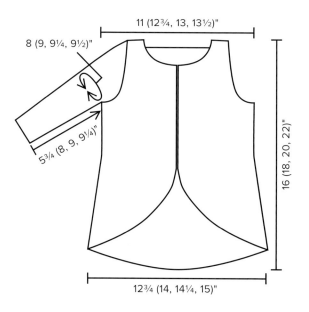

11 (12¾, 13, 13½)"

8 (9, 9¼, 9½)"

5¾ (8, 9, 9¼)"

16 (18, 20, 22)"

12¾ (14, 14¼, 15)"

Bite This Book!

When my son, Felix, was a baby, he had a basket bursting with soft books. This knitted picture book, featuring bold shapes and bright colors, is my own version. Each page is only 30 stitches wide and 40 rows long: A great opportunity for you to play with intarsia. Dream up a story about a funny red dog in a lavender sky, or invent a narrative for any of the other quirky images. Baby can read along—or just chew on a corner.

DESIGNED BY KAT COYLE

Finished Measurements

• • •

Each page is 5½" (14cm) square

Materials

• • •

Tahki Cotton Classic, 100% Mercerized Cotton, [108yd (99m) per 50g skein]; 1 skein each color

#3995 Red
#3407 Rust
#3351 Peach
#3559 Yellow Ochre

#3760 Light Green
#3763 Bright Green
#3774 Chrome Green
#3805 Aqua
#3803 Light Blue
#3856 Navy Blue
#3940 Purple
#3936 Lavender
#3002 Black
#3001 White

Note: *Only a very small amount of #3001 White is used. Embroidery thread may be substituted if desired.*

For a list of the colors used for each page, see the pattern.

1 set US #4 (3.5mm) straight needles

1 F-5 (3.75mm) crochet hook

Bobbins

Yarn needle

Gauge

• • •

21 stitches and 31 rows = 4" (10cm) in stockinette stitch

INTARSIA

To work a motif using this technique, work each area of color from a separate strand of that color. The yarn not in use is not stranded across the back of the work. To prepare for working an intarsia design, wind a few small balls or bobbins of each color.

When you come to a point in the pattern where you need to change colors, drop the old color and pick up the strand of the new color from underneath the old color, so that the strands are twisted at the point where the two colors meet. This will prevent holes from forming at these points.

Check suggested reading list and websites on page 142 for resources.

DUPLICATE STITCH

Duplicate stitch produces the same effect of a knitted-in design by duplicating the path taken by the yarn in a knitted stitch. On the right side of the work, a knit stitch has a "V" shape. Beginning at the base of this V, bring the needle up through the work. At the top right corner of the V, bring the needle back down through the work. Bring the needle behind the work to the upper left corner of the V, and draw it up through the work. At the base of the V, bring the needle back down through the work. One duplicate stitch is complete.

The long-tail cast-on is recommended for this project.

BOOK

• • •

The pages of this book are worked in stockinette stitch, using the intarsia technique of colorwork.

For each page, cast on 30 stitches using the color indicated.

The colors used for each page are as follows:

Bird: #3774 Chrome Green, #3002 Black, #3559 Yellow Ochre
Cast on using #3774 Chrome Green.

Cat: #3774 Chrome Green, #3803 Light Blue, #3940 Purple, #3936 Lavender
Cast on using #3774 Chrome Green.

Dog: #3936 Lavender, #3995 Red, #3559 Yellow Ochre
Cast on using #3936 Lavender.

Fish: #3856 Navy Blue, #3805 Aqua, #3760 Light Green, #3763 Bright Green
Cast on using #3856 Navy Blue.

Moon: #3856 Navy Blue, #3803 Light Blue, #3001 White
Cast on using #3856 Navy Blue.

Sun: #3351 Peach, #3407 Rust, #3559 Yellow Ochre
Cast on using #3407 Rust.

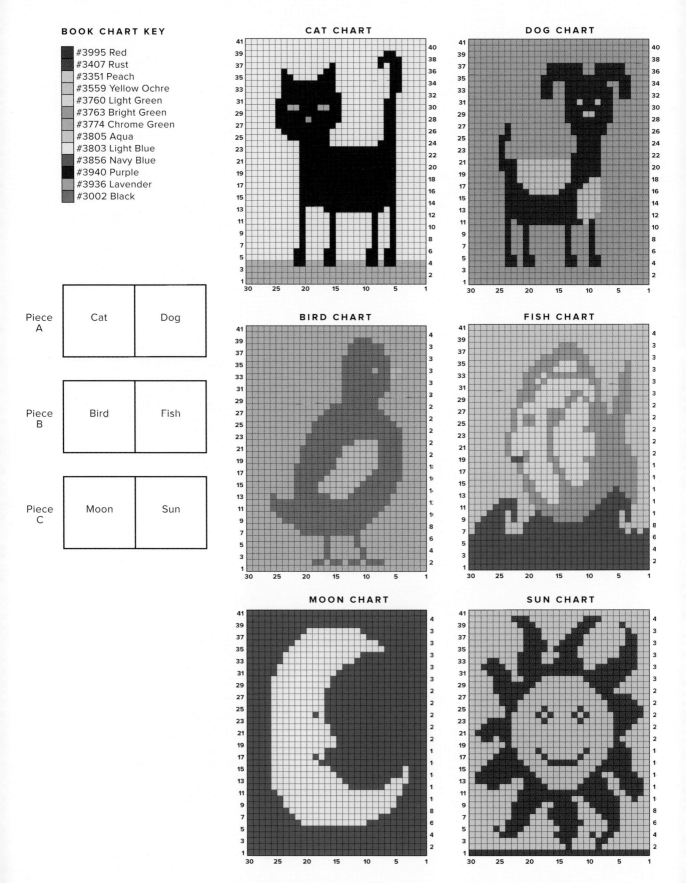

BOOK CHART KEY

- #3995 Red
- #3407 Rust
- #3351 Peach
- #3559 Yellow Ochre
- #3760 Light Green
- #3763 Bright Green
- #3774 Chrome Green
- #3805 Aqua
- #3803 Light Blue
- #3856 Navy Blue
- #3940 Purple
- #3936 Lavender
- #3002 Black

Piece A	Cat	Dog

Piece B	Bird	Fish

Piece C	Moon	Sun

CAT CHART

DOG CHART

BIRD CHART

FISH CHART

MOON CHART

SUN CHART

Purl 1 row; this is Row 1 of the chart.

Work rows 2–41 of the chart.
In places where only a few stitches of one color are worked (the face of the Sun and the face of the Fish), work those stitches using the background color for that section, then work those stitches in duplicate stitch during the finishing process.

Bind off all stitches, using the color used in row 41. Cut the yarn, leaving a long tail.

Finishing
• • •

Using the photo on page 63 as a guide, embroider small stars on the Moon page using White.
Embroider a pupil in the eye of the Fish using Navy Blue yarn.
Work duplicate stitch as necessary to fill in details.

Weave in ends, using yarn tails to fix any holes or irregularities in the colorwork.

Immerse all pages in lukewarm water and allow them to soak until they are thoroughly saturated. Gently squeeze the water out (do not wring!) and lay the pages on top of several towels on a flat surface. Carefully pin them out to the dimensions given. Allow them to dry completely.

ASSEMBLY
• • •

Mattress stitch the edges of the pages together as shown in the diagrams (to left of charts).
Ensuring that the tops of all the pages are facing the same direction, lay Piece A on a table with the right side facing down.
Lay Piece B on Piece A, with the right side facing up; the wrong sides of Pieces A and B are together.
Finally, lay Piece C on top of Piece B, with the right side facing down. The right sides of Pieces B and C are together.

Use the red yarn to sew all the pieces together through their centers, taking care to sew through the seam that joins each piece. Tie the ends of this yarn into a bow.

Use the red yarn to whipstich around the edges of the pages as follows:
Sew the Dog and Bird pages together, the Sun and Moon pages together, and the Fish and Cat pages.

Weave in any remaining ends.
• • •

Big Idea Vest

Is your kid a budding bookworm? Throw this BIG vest over a buttoned-down shirt and he'll be cool for school. The cushy yarn works up quickly on big needles using a simple stockinette stitch; because some of the stripes are only one row wide, circular needles are used to work from both ends. The design requires minimal shaping or finishing. Smart stripes in neutrals and neon green are a dapper finishing touch. Single crochet edging along the V-neck and around the armholes pulls it all together.

DESIGNED BY EDNA HART

Finished Sizes and Measurements

• • •

6–12 months (12–18 months, 18–24 months, 2–3 years, 3–4 years)
Shown in size 3–4 years

Note: *This pattern is written to provide considerable ease. If you prefer a closer fit, check the measurements and choose a smaller size.*

Chest: 21½ (24, 26, 28½, 31)"
(54.6 [61, 66, 72, 79]cm)

Length: 13 (14, 15, 16, 17)"
(33 [35.5, 38, 40.5, 43]cm)

Materials

• • •

Blue Sky Alpaca Cotton [100% Cotton; 150 yd/ 137 m per 100 g skein]; 1 skein each color

[MC] #613 Ink

[CC1] #614 Drift

[CC2] #625 Graphite

[CC3] #607 Lemongrass

[CC4] #626 Stone

[CC5] #605 Cumin

1 US 10.5 (6.5mm) circular needle, 16" (40cm) or longer

1 US J-10 (6mm) crochet hook

Yarn needle

Stitch holder

Gauge

• • •

14 stitches and 18 rows = 4" (10cm) in stockinette stitch

• • • STITCH STORY • • •

1X1 RIB
Row 1 (RS): *K1, p1, repeat from * to last 2 stitches, k2.
Row 2 (WS): P2, *k1, p1, repeat from * to end.

STRIPE SEQUENCE
1 Row MC (Ink)
2 Rows CC1 (Drift)
1 Row MC (Ink)
4 Rows CC2 (Graphite)

1 Row MC (Ink)
2 Rows CC1 (Drift)
1 Row MC (Ink)
4 Rows CC3 (Lemongrass)
1 Row MC (Ink)
2 Rows CC1 (Drift)
1 Row MC (Ink)
4 Rows CC4 (Stone)
1 Row MC (Ink)
2 Rows CC1 (Drift)
1 Row MC (Ink)
4 Rows CC5 (Cumin)
Repeat these 32 rows for stripe sequence.
Carry MC and CC1 along the side of the work when not in use. At times, when working the stripe pattern, you will find that the yarn you need is attached to the opposite end of the work from where your last row ended; to work the next stripe, slide the work to the other end of the needle. This will mean that you will sometimes end up working 2 consecutive right side rows or wrong side rows.

• • •

VEST
• • •

BACK
• •

Using MC, cast on 38 (42, 46, 50, 54) stitches.
Do not join work.
Work 2 rows in 1x1 rib.

From this point, the Back is worked entirely in stockinette stitch, in stripe pattern.
Work until the piece measures 8 (8½, 9, 9½, 10)" (20.5 [21.5, 23, 24, 25.5]cm), ending with a wrong side row.

Shape Armholes
Bind off 2 (2, 2, 4, 4) stitches at the beginning of the next 2 rows. 34 (38, 42, 42, 46) stitches.

Continue in stockinette stitch until the work measures 12 (13, 14, 15, 16)" (30.5 [33, 35.5, 38, 40.5]cm), ending with a wrong side row.

Next Row (RS): K7 (8, 10, 10, 11) and place these stitches on a stitch holder, bind off next 20 (22, 22, 22, 24) stitches, knit to end. 7 (8, 10, 10, 11) stitches.

Work 3 rows in stockinette stitch.
Bind off all stitches.

Replace the held stitches on the needle with the wrong side facing, and reattach the yarn.
Work 3 rows in stockinette stitch.
Bind off all stitches.

FRONT
• •

Cast on and work as for the Back up to the beginning of the armhole shaping. Be sure to end at the same point in the stripe sequence as you did for the Back.

Shape Armholes
Bind off 2 (2, 2, 4, 4) stitches at the beginning of the next 2 rows. 34 (38, 42, 42, 46) stitches.

Work 2 rows in stockinette stitch. The next row worked must be a right side row; if necessary, work an extra row before proceeding.

Shape Neckline
Note: *Because of the way the stripe pattern is worked, shaping rows may be worked on either right side rows or wrong side rows. Because of this, instructions for both right side and wrong side shaping rows will be given.*

Next Row (RS): K15 (17, 19, 19, 21), k2tog; place the remaining 17 (19, 21, 21, 23) stitches on a stitch holder.

Note: For this half of the neckline shaping, shaping rows will be worked as follows:
Right Side Shaping Row: *Knit to last 2 stitches, k2tog.*
Wrong Side Shaping Row: *P2tog, purl to end.*

Work 1 row in stockinette stitch.
Work 1 shaping row.
Repeat these 2 rows 8 (9, 9, 9, 10) times more. 7 (8, 10, 10, 11) stitches.

Continue in stockinette stitch until the piece measures the same as the Back to the shoulder.
Bind off all stitches.

Replace the held stitches on the needle with the right side facing, and rejoin the yarn.

Next Row (RS): Ssk, knit to end.

For this half of the neckline shaping, shaping rows will be worked as follows:
Right Side Shaping Row: *Ssk, knit to end.*
Wrong Side Shaping Row: *Purl to last 2 stitches, p2tog tbl.*

Work 1 row in stockinette stitch.
Work 1 shaping row.
Repeat these 2 rows 8 (9, 9, 9, 10) times more.
7 (8, 10, 10, 11) stitches.

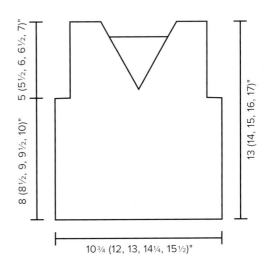

5 (5½, 6, 6½, 7)"

8 (8½, 9, 9½, 10)"

13 (14, 15, 16, 17)"

10¾ (12, 13, 14¼, 15½)"

Continue in stockinette stitch until the piece measures the same as the Back to the shoulder.
Bind off all stitches.

Finishing

• • •

Weave in all ends.
Immerse the pieces in lukewarm water and allow them to soak until they are thoroughly saturated. Gently squeeze out the water (do not wring!) and lay the pieces on top of several towels on a flat surface. Carefully pin them out to the dimensions given. Allow them to dry completely.

Sew the Back and Front together at the shoulders and sides, matching the stripes at the side seams.

Using MC, work 1 round of single crochet around the armhole edges.

Work 1 round of single crochet around the neckline edge.
Work a second round of single crochet, but do not work into the center stitch of the V at the center front of the neckline.

Weave in the remaining ends.

• • •

At the Gallery

Surreal or pop, abstract or figurative, insider or outsider—whatever your taste in art, there's plenty of inspiration to be found at the gallery. Stitch up a whole world of artful knitwear, including a colorful Painter's Smock and Beret and Petite Beat Bonnets that'll suit a troupe of wee performance artists. It's opening night at the gallery: Time to invite all budding *artistes* and visionaries out to play.

Painter's Smock and Beret

Perfect for your favorite little artist, this loose-fitting sweater features the comfortable shape of a painter's smock and a matching beret. Warm fauvist colors of mangoes and palms bring the ensemble to life. Striped cuffs and a yoke in garter stitch, patch pockets, and a Peter Pan collar complete the picture. With its generous gauge, this set is relatively quick to make, so your aspiring painter can be at her easel in no time. (Washable markers won't limit her creativity one bit.)

DESIGNED BY KAT COYLE

Finished Sizes and Measurements

• • •

6–12 months (1–2 years, 2–3 years, 3–4 years)
Shown in size 2–3 years

SMOCK

Chest: 23½ (28, 32, 36)" (59.5 [71, 81, 91]cm)

Length: 13 (15, 16½, 18¼)" (33 [38, 42, 46.4]cm)

BERET

Brim circumference *(unstretched)*: 12¾ (13¾, 15, 16)" (32.5 [35, 38, 40.5]cm)

Materials

• • •

Crystal Palace Yarns Merino Frappe, 80% Wool / 20% Polyamide, [140yd (130m) per 50g ball]

SMOCK

[MC] #061 Toffee; 3 (3, 4, 4) balls

[CC1] #014 Crocus; 1 (1, 1, 2) balls

[CC2] #016 Fern; 1 ball

[CC3] #029B New Sorbet; 1 ball

BERET

1 ball is required of each color, unless you make the smock, in which case you will be able to make the beret using your leftover yarn.

[MC] #061 Toffee

[CC1] #014 Crocus

[CC2] #016 Fern

1 US #8 (5mm) circular needle, 24" (60cm) or longer (Smock only)

One 16" (40cm) US #8 (5mm) circular needle (Beret only)

1 set US #8 (5mm) double-pointed needles

Stitch holders

Yarn needle

Sewing needle and thread

Three ⅞" (22mm) buttons

Gauge

• • •

15 stitches and 24 rows = 4" (10cm) in stockinette stitch

••• STITCH STORY •••

WRAP AND TURN
Note: Used when working short rows.

Knit to point specified in pattern, slip next stitch to right-hand needle, bring yarn to front of work between needles, slip stitch back to left-hand needle, turn work to begin knitting back in the other direction.

GARTER STITCH IN THE ROUND
Round 1: Knit
Round 2: Purl

• • •

SMOCK
• • •

LOWER BODY
• •

Using the longer circular needle and CC2, cast on 98 (114, 130, 146) stitches.
Row 1 (RS): K5, place marker, k22 (26, 30, 34), place marker, k44 (52, 60, 68), place marker, k22 (26, 30, 34), place marker, k5.
Row 2: Knit all stitches.
Rows 3–10: Using CC1, knit all stitches.
Rows 11–16: Using CC3, knit all stitches.
Rows 17–18: Using CC1, knit all stitches. Border is complete.

Note: Read ahead about the placement of button-holes before proceeding.

Work as follows, using MC:
Next Row (RS): Knit all stitches.
Next Row (WS): K5, purl to last marker, k5.
Repeat these 2 rows until the work measures 7½ (9, 10, 11 ¼)" (19 [23, 25.5, 28.5]cm), ending with a wrong side row.

At the same time, when the work measures 5½ (6½, 6¾, 7¾)" (14 [16.5, 17.2, 19.7]cm), work a buttonhole as follows:

Buttonhole Row 1 (RS): K2, bind off 2 stitches, knit to end.
Buttonhole Row 2 (WS): Work in pattern to last marker, k1, cast on 2 stitches, k2.

While working the body of the Smock as follows, work a second buttonhole when the work measures 7½ (9, 9¾, 11)" (19 [23, 24.7, 28]cm).
Work a third buttonhole when the work measures 9½ (11½, 12¾, 14¼)" (24 [29.2, 32.5, 36.2]cm).

Divide for Armholes
When the work measures 7½ (9, 10, 11¼)" (19 [23, 25.5, 28.5]cm), ending with a wrong side row, work as follows:

Next Row (RS): Knit to 2 (2, 3, 3) stitches before second marker, place all stitches just worked on a stitch holder; bind off 4 (4, 6, 6) stitches and remove marker, knit to end.
Next Row (WS): K5, purl to 2 (2, 3, 3) stitches before second marker, place all stitches just worked on a stitch holder; bind off 4 (4, 6, 6) stitches and remove marker, purl to end.
The upper Back will be worked over the remaining 40 (48, 54, 62) stitches.

BACK
• •

Bind off 2 (2, 2, 3) stitches at the beginning of the next 2 rows. 36 (44, 50, 56) stitches.

Next Row (RS): K1, ssk, knit to last 3 stitches, k2tog, k1.
Purl 1 row.
Repeat these 2 rows 1 (2, 3, 4) times more. 32 (38, 42, 46) stitches.

Work 2 (2, 2, 4) rows in stockinette stitch.

Back Yoke
Size 6–12 months only:
Row 1 (RS): Using CC2, k9, k2tog, k10, k2tog, k9.
30 stitches.

Sizes 1–2 years, 2–3 years, 3–4 years only:
Row 1 (RS): Using CC2, k – (10, 12, 13), k3tog, k – (12, 12, 14), k3tog, k – (10, 12, 13). – (34, 38, 42) stitches.

All Sizes:
Rows 2–4: Using CC2, knit all stitches.
Rows 5–12: Using CC1, knit all stitches.
Rows 13–18: Using CC3, knit all stitches.
Rows 19–22: Using CC1, knit all stitches.

Continuing in garter stitch with CC1, shape the shoulders as follows:
Bind off 4 (5, 6, 6) stitches at the beginning of the next 2 rows. 22 (24, 26, 30) stitches.
Bind off 4 (4, 5, 5) stitches at the beginning of the next 2 rows.
Bind off the remaining 14 (16, 16, 20) stitches.

LEFT FRONT
• •

Replace the held 25 (29, 32, 36) stitches of the Left Front on the needle with the right side facing, and join MC at the armhole edge.

Row 1 (RS): Bind off 2 (2, 2, 3) stitches, knit to end. 23 (27, 30, 33) stitches.
Row 2 (WS): K5, purl to end.

Row 3 (RS): K1, ssk, knit to end.
Row 4 (WS): K5, purl to end.
Repeat the last 2 rows 1 (2, 3, 4) times more. 21 (24, 26, 28) stitches.

Work 2 (2, 2, 4) rows in stockinette stitch.

Yoke
Note: Read ahead before proceeding. Yoke patterning and neckline shaping are worked at the same time.

Row 1 (RS): Using CC2, k4 (4, 5, 7), k3tog, k4 (4, 5, 7), k3tog, k7 (10, 10, 8). 17 (20, 22, 24) stitches.
Work Rows 2–22 as for back yoke.

At the same time, beginning on Row 12 (10, 10, 6) of yoke (a wrong side row), shape neckline as follows:

Bind off 5 stitches, knit to end. 12 (15, 17, 19) stitches.

Next Row (RS): Knit to last 3 stitches, k2tog, k1.
Knit 1 row.
Repeat these 2 rows 3 (5, 5, 7) times more. 8 (9, 11, 11) stitches remain.

When all 22 rows of the yoke pattern have been worked, shape the shoulder as follows:

Next Row (RS): Bind off 4 (5, 6, 6) stitches, knit to end.
Knit 1 row.
Bind off the remaining 4 (4, 5, 5) stitches.

RIGHT FRONT

• •

Replace the held 25 (29, 32, 36) stitches of the Right Front on the needle with the wrong side facing, and join MC at the armhole edge.

Row 1 (WS): Bind off 2 (2, 2, 3) stitches, purl to last 5 stitches, k5. 23 (27, 30, 33) stitches.

Row 2 (RS): Knit to last 3 stitches, k2tog, k1.
Row 3 (WS): Purl to last 5 stitches, k5.
Repeat Rows 2 and 3 again 1 (2, 3, 4) times. 21 (24, 26, 28) stitches.

Work 4 (4, 4, 6) rows in stockinette stitch.

Yoke

Note: *Read ahead before proceeding. Yoke patterning and neckline shaping are worked at the same time.*

Row 1 (RS): Using CC2, k7 (10, 10, 8), k3tog, k4 (4, 5, 7), k3tog, k4 (4, 5, 7). 17 (20, 22, 24) stitches.
Work Rows 2–22 as for back yoke.

At the same time, beginning on Row 11 (9, 9, 5) of yoke (a right side row), shape neckline as follows:

Bind off 5 stitches, knit to end. 12 (15, 17, 19) stitches.

Knit 1 row.
Next Row (RS): Knit to last 3 stitches, k2tog, k1.

Repeat these 2 rows 3 (5, 5, 7) times more. 8 (9, 11, 11) stitches remain.

When all 22 rows of the yoke pattern have been worked, shape the shoulder as follows:

Knit 1 row.
Next Row (WS): Bind off 4 (5, 6, 6) stitches, knit to end.
Knit 1 row.
Bind off the remaining 4 (4, 5, 5) stitches.

SLEEVES

• •

Sew Fronts to Back at shoulders.

Using double-pointed needles and MC, with the right side facing and beginning at the center of one bound-off underarm edge, pick up and knit 2 (2, 3, 3) stitches along one half of the initial underarm bind-off, pick up and knit 2 (2, 2, 3) stitches in the next row of bound-off stitches, pick up and knit 5 (6, 8, 10) stitches along the edge of the MC section to the lower edge of the yoke, pick up and knit 22 stitches (1 stitch in each garter ridge) along the front and back edges of the yoke, pick up and knit 5 (6, 8, 10) stitches along the edge of the MC section to the lower edge of the armhole, pick up and knit 4 (4, 5, 6) stitches in the remaining bound-off stitches to the center of the underarm. 40 (42, 48, 54) stitches. Join to begin working in the round.

Knit 6 rounds.

Next Round: Ssk, knit to last 2 stitches, k2tog.
Knit 7 rounds.
Repeat these 8 rounds 4 (4, 5, 7) times more.
30 (32, 36, 38) stitches.

Knit until the Sleeve measures 7¼ (8¼, 9½, 11)"
(18.5 [21, 24, 28]cm), or 2¼" (5.5cm) less than the
desired length.

Cuff
Sizes 6–12 months and 2–3 years only:
Round 1: Using CC1, *k1, k2tog, repeat from * to end.
20 (– , 24, –) stitches.

Sizes 1–2 years and 3–4 years only:
Round 1: Using CC1, k2tog, *k1, k2tog, repeat from * to
end. – (21, – , 25) stitches.

All Sizes:
Round 2: Using CC1, purl all stitches.

Rounds 3–8: Work in garter stitch using CC3.
Rounds 9–14: Work in garter stitch using CC1.
Rounds 15–16: Work in garter stitch using CC2.
Bind off all stitches.

Work the other Sleeve in the same way.

COLLAR
• •

Using the circular needle and CC1, with the right side
facing and beginning at the Right Front neckline edge,
just after the bound-off stitches of the buttonhole band,
pick up and knit 11 (13, 13, 15) stitches along the Right
Front neckline edge, 14 (16, 16, 20) stitches along the
Back neckline edge, and 11 (13, 13, 15) stitches along the
Left Front neckline edge, to the edge of the button band.
36 (42, 42, 50) stitches.
Knit 22 (22, 22, 24) rows.

Shape collar as follows:
Row 1: Ssk, k8 (8, 8, 10) wrap and turn, knit to end.
Row 2: Ssk, k6 (6, 6, 8) wrap and turn, knit to end.
Row 3: Ssk, k4 (4, 4, 6) wrap and turn, knit to end.
Row 4: Ssk, knit to end. 18 (18, 18, 20) stitches.

Repeat Rows 1–3 for other side of collar.
Last Row: Ssk, bind off all stitches.

POCKETS (MAKE 2)
• •

Using CC1, cast on 11 stitches.
Row 1 (RS): K1, m1, knit to last stitch, m1, k1.
Row 2 (WS): Knit all stitches.
Repeat these 2 rows twice more. 15 stitches.

Using CC3, knit 6 rows.
Using CC1, knit 2 rows.
Using MC, work 10 rows in stockinette stitch, working
2 stitches at each edge in garter stitch and beginning
with a right side row.
Using CC2, knit 2 rows. Bind off all stitches.

Finishing
• • •

Sew the Pockets to the front of the sweater, matching
the stripes on the Pockets to the stripes on the lower
border of the Sweater.

Weave in all ends.
Lightly block the sweater.
Sew the buttons to the buttonhole band, opposite
the buttonholes.

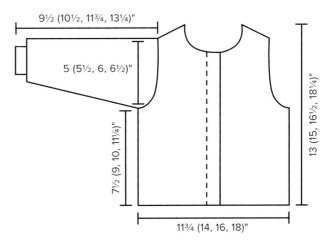

9½ (10½, 11¾, 13¼)"

5 (5½, 6, 6½)"

7½ (9, 10, 11¼)"

13 (15, 16½, 18¼)"

11¾ (14, 16, 18)"

Using MC, knit 3 rounds.
Next Round: *K3, k2tog, repeat from * to end.
48 (52, 56, 60) stitches.

Using CC1, work 2 rounds in garter stitch.

Using MC, knit 2 rounds.
Next Round: *K2, k2tog, repeat from * to end.
36 (39, 42, 45) stitches.
Knit 1 round.

Using CC1, work 2 rounds in garter stitch.

Next Round: Using MC, *k1, k2tog, repeat from * to end. 24 (26, 28, 30) stitches.
Knit 3 rounds.

Next Round: Using CC1, (k2tog) to end. 12 (13, 14, 15) stitches.
Purl 1 round.

Using MC, knit 1 round.
Next Round: K0 (1, 0, 1), (k2tog) to end. 6 (7, 7, 8) stitches.
Next Round: K0 (1, 1, 0), (k2tog) to end. 3 (4, 4, 4) stitches.

BERET

• • •

Using CC2 and double-pointed needles, cast on 48 (52, 56, 60) stitches. Divide stitches evenly between needles and join to begin working in the round, being careful not to twist the stitches.
Work 3 rounds in garter stitch, beginning with a purl round.
Using CC1, work 2 rounds in garter stitch.

Next Round: Using MC and switching to short circular needle if desired, *k2, m1, repeat from * to end. 72 (78, 84, 90) stitches.
Work in stockinette stitch until the work measures 2¾ (3, 3½, 3½)" (7 [7.5, 9, 9]cm) from the last CC1 round.

Shape top of beret as follows, switching back to double-pointed needles when necessary:

Next Round: Using CC1, *k4, k2tog, repeat from * to end. 60 (65, 70, 75) stitches.
Purl 1 round.

Slip the remaining stitches to one needle so that the last stitch of the last round is at the end of the needle.
Work I-Cord as follows:
Instead of turning the work around to work back on the wrong side, slide all stitches to the other end of the needle, transfer the needle to your left hand, bring the yarn around the back of the work, and start knitting the stitches again.
Repeat this row twice
Bind off all stitches.

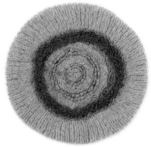

Finishing

• • •

Weave in all ends.

• • •

Patchwork Dreamer

Here's an ingenious way for knitters to recreate the wonderful graphic quality of traditional quilts in a knitted form. This version of the log cabin design is a good remedy for any quilting urges. The best part? There isn't any sewing involved; the patches are simply knit together by picking up stitches along a finished edge. With baby in mind, the yarn chosen for this blanket is remarkably snuggly and the colors wonderfully bold.

DESIGNED BY EDNA HART

Finished Measurements

• • •

Width: Approximately 28" (71cm)

Length: Approximately 36" (91cm)

Materials

• • •

Trendsetter Zucca, 58% Tactel / 42% Polyamid, [71yd (65m) per 50g ball]

[MC]: #5115 Paprika; 2 balls

[CC1]: #5118 Sea; 2 balls

[CC2]: #5135 Neon; 3 balls

[CC3]: #5008 Spice; 2 balls

2 US 10.5/6.5mm circular needles, each at least 29" (74cm) long

Yarn needle

Gauge

• • •

13 stitches / 20 rows = 4" (10 cm) in garter stitch

Pattern Notes

• • •

Fabric knitted in this yarn is difficult to unravel because of its fluffy texture. Be careful when picking up stitches and be sure to work under a good light.

This pattern is worked back and forth using circular needles to hold the large numbers of stitches involved in later steps.

BLANKET

• • •

Note: *The blanket is worked in garter stitch throughout.*

Section 1

Using MC, cast on 28 stitches. Knit 15 rows. Bind off all stitches.

Section 2

Using CC1, pick up and knit 10 stitches along one short edge of the work.

Knit 15 rows. Bind off all stitches.

Repeat Section 2 along the opposite short edge of the work.

Section 3

Using CC2, pick up and knit 44 stitches along one long edge of the work.
Knit 15 rows. Bind off all stitches.

Repeat Section 3 along the opposite long edge of the work.

Section 4

Using CC3, pick up and knit 30 stitches along one short edge of the work.
Knit 15 rows. Bind off all stitches.

Repeat Section 4 along the opposite short edge of the work.

Section 5

Using MC, pick up and knit 70 stitches along one long edge of the work.
Knit 2 rows. Cut MC.
Using CC1, knit 15 rows. Bind off all stitches.

Repeat Section 5 along the opposite long edge of the work.

Section 6

Using CC2, pick up and knit 48 stitches along one short edge of the work.
Knit 15 rows. Bind off all stitches.

Repeat Section 6 along the opposite short edge of the work.

Section 7

Using MC, pick up and knit 88 stitches along one long edge of the work.
Knit 2 rows. Cut MC.
Using CC3, knit 15 rows. Bind off all stitches.

Repeat Section 7 along the opposite long edge of the work.

Section 8

Using CC1, pick up and knit 64 stitches along one short edge of the work.

Knit 15 rows. Bind off all stitches.

Repeat Section 8 along the opposite short edge of the work.

Section 9

Using MC, pick up and knit 108 stitches along one long edge of the work.
Knit 2 rows. Cut MC.
Using CC2, knit 15 rows. Bind off all stitches.

Repeat Section 9 along the opposite long edge of the work.

Edging

Using MC and one circular needle, pick up and knit 80 stitches along one short edge of the work, pick up 2 stitches in corner, pick up 108 stitches along the adjacent long edge; using the second needle, pick up stitches along the remaining edges in the same way.

Join to begin working in the round, and knit 1 round.
Purl 1 round.
Bind off all stitches very loosely.

Finishing

• • •

Weave in all ends.

• • •

Modernist Stripe Sleep Sacque

The sleep sacque, a kind of nightgown and sleeping bag rolled into one, keeps tiny dreamers snuggly. A striped carnival wheel of color, the gown is worked in the round from the bottom hem edge to the neck, while the set-in sleeves are worked separately and seamed to the body. With lapped shoulders and encased elastic at the bottom, you'll be able to change your drowsy darling with ease. The large pocket at the chest is a perfect place to stash a small stuffed pal: See the matching mobile pattern on page 87 for some charming options.

DESIGNED BY MARY-HEATHER COGAR

Finished Sizes and Measurements

• • •

0–3 months (3–6 months, 6–9 months, 9–12 months)
Shown in size 3–6 months

Chest: 17 (18.5, 20, 21)" (45.5 [47, 51, 53.5]cm)

Length: 19½ (21¾, 23¾, 26)" (49.5 [55.2, 60.3, 66]cm)

Materials

• • •

Brown Sheep Cotton Fleece, 80% Pima Cotton / 20% Wool, [215yd (195m) per 100g skein]

[MC] #CW710 Prosperous Plum; 2 (2, 3, 3) skeins

[CC1] #CW765 Blue Paradise; 1 skein

[CC2] #CW810 Cherry Moon; 1 skein

[CC3] #CW840 Lime Light; 1 skein

[CC4] # CW725 Buttercream; 1 skein

[CC5] #CW625 Terracotta Canyon; 1 skein

One 16" (40cm) US #4 (3.5mm) circular needle

1 set US #4 (3.5mm) straight needles

1 E-4 (3.5mm) crochet hook

Stitch markers

Stitch holder

Yarn needle

1 package ¼" (6mm) elastic

Sewing needle and white thread to sew elastic band together

Gauge

• • •

21 stitches and 30 rows = 4" (10cm)

M1L (Make 1 Left): Insert the left needle from front to back, under the horizontal strand that lies between the stitch just knit and the next stitch. Knit this stitch through its back loop.

M1R (Make 1 Right): Insert the left needle from back to front, under the horizontal strand that lies between the stitch just knit and the next stitch. Knit this stitch through its front loop.

STRIPE PATTERN

Work 4 rows using CC2. Work 6 rows using MC.
Work 4 rows using CC3. Work 6 rows using MC.
Work 4 rows using CC4. Work 6 rows using MC.
Work 4 rows using CC5. Work 6 rows using MC.
Work 4 rows using CC1. Work 6 rows using MC.
Repeat these 50 rows until Body is complete.

• • •

1, 2, 3, 4, 5, 6, 7,
Using MC Knit 5 rounds
✓✓✓✓
Work in Stripe pattern
to 17 in.

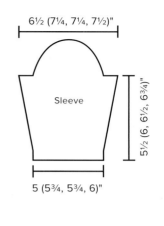

6½ (7¼, 7¼, 7½)"

Sleeve

5½ (6, 6½, 6¾)"

5 (5¾, 5¾, 6)"

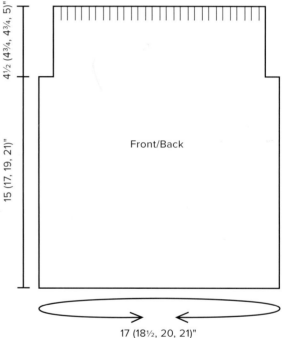

4½ (4¾, 4¾, 5)"

15 (17, 19, 21)"

Front/Back

17 (18½, 20, 21)"

Round 5: Knit around, knitting first stitch of the double yarn over and allowing the extra wrap to drop.
Round 6: Knit all stitches.
Round 7: Purl all stitches. This round forms a turning ridge for the hem.
The hem facing is now complete. Cut CC1.

Using MC, knit 5 rounds.

Fold the hem facing along the turning ridge to the inside of the work. The wrong sides of the hem facing and hem are together, and the cast-on edge is directly behind the stitches on the needle. In the next round, you will join the hem and hem facing.

Next Round: *Insert the tip of the left needle into the stitch of the cast-on edge that is directly behind the first stitch on the needle. Knit this stitch together with the first stitch on the needle. Repeat from * until all stitches have been worked.

As the hem facing is slightly longer than the outside of the hem, it will appear slightly puffy at this point. The hem forms the casing for the drawstring or elastic that will be insterted later; once it is inserted, this effect will be mitigated.

Continuing in stockinette stitch, work in stripe pattern until the work measures 15 (17, 19, 21)" (38 [43, 48.5, 53.5]cm).

Divide for Armholes

Dividing Round: *Knit to 2 (2, 3, 3) stitches before marker, bind off next 4 (4, 6, 6) stitches, removing marker, repeat from * once.

Knit 41 (45, 47, 49) stitches; place the remaining 41 (45, 47, 49) stitches on a stitch holder for back.

Upper Front

Working back and forth, continue in stripe pattern until the work measures 3 (3¼, 3¼, 3½)" (7.5 [8.2, 8.2, 9]cm) from the dividing round, ending with a wrong side row. Cut the yarn.

Neck Ribbing

Row 1 (RS): Using CC1, knit all stitches.
Row 2 (WS): P1, *k1, p1, repeat from * to end.
Row 3 (RS): K1, *p1, k1, repeat from * to end.
Repeat Rows 2 and 3 until ribbing measures 1½" (3.8cm), ending with a wrong side row. Bind off all stitches in pattern.

Replace the held stitches on the needle and work the upper back in the same way as the upper front.

SLEEVES (MAKE 2)
• •

Using straight needles and CC1, cast on 26 (30, 30, 32) stitches.
Row 1 (RS): K2, *p1, k1, repeat from * to end.
Row 2 (WS): *P1, k1, repeat from * to last 2 stitches, p2.
Repeat these 2 rows 1 (1, 2, 2) times more. Cut CC1.

Using MC, work as follows:
Increase Row (RS): K1, M1R, knit to last stitch, M1L, k1.
Work 9 rows in stockinette stitch.
Repeat these 10 rows 3 times more. 34 (38, 38, 40) stitches.

Continue in stockinette stitch until the work measures 5½ (6, 6½, 6¾)" (14 [15, 16.5, 17.2]cm).

Shape Sleeve Cap
Bind off 2 (2, 3, 3) stitches at the beginning of the next 2 rows. 30 (34, 32, 34) stitches.

Decrease Row (RS): K2, ssk, knit to last 4 stitches, k2tog, k2.
Purl 1 row.
Repeat these 2 rows 8 (7, 8, 8) times more.
12 (18, 14, 16) stitches.

Work Decrease Row as above.
Next Row (WS): P2, p2tog, purl to last 4 stitches, p2tog tbl, p2.

Size 3–6 months only:
Repeat the last 2 rows once more.

All Sizes:
Bind off the remaining 8 (10, 10, 12) stitches.

POCKET
• •

Using CC1 and straight needles, cast on 29 stitches.
Purl 1 row.
Increase Row (RS): K1, M1R, knit to last stitch, M1L, k1.
Work 3 rows in stockinette stitch.
Work Increase Row.
Continue in stockinette stitch until the work measures 3½" (9cm) ending with a right side row.

Next Row (WS): P1, *k1, p1, repeat from * to end.
Next Row (RS): K1, *p1, k1, repeat from * to end.
Repeat these 2 rows 3 times more.
Bind off all stitches in pattern.

Finishing
• • •

Lap the back ribbing over the front ribbing, so that the top edge of the back ribbing touches the lower edge of the front ribbing. Sew the ribbed bands together along their side edges.

Sew the sleeve seams.
Sew the sleeves into the armholes.

Sew the pocket to the upper front, using the photo as a guide.
Weave in all ends.

Elastic
Cut a piece of ¼"- (6mm-) wide elastic that is 15" (38cm) long, or 1" (2.5cm) longer than the desired measurement.
Insert the elastic into the casing, ensuring that it does not twist.
Overlap the ends of the elastic by 1" (2.5cm), and sew the ends together securely.
• • •

Mobile Menagerie

Babies adore the colors and movement of mobiles, and parents love how they lull babies to sleep or provide distraction during diaper changes. Toddlers will also love this whimsical mobile, with six characters that form a garden menagerie: A giant ladybug, smiling sun, puffy dragonfly, plump bee, blue inchworm, and a bright butterfly—all hovering in a constellation of color. The added bonus: Each soft creature is easily detached for baby to play with.

DESIGNED BY MARY-HEATHER COGAR

Materials

• • •

Brown Sheep Cotton Fleece, 80% Pima Cotton / 20% Wool, [215yd (195m)] per 100g skein], 1 skein each color

[MC] #CW145 Black Forest

[CC1] #CW765 Blue Paradise

[CC2] #CW840 Lime Light

[CC3] #CW710 Prosperous Plum

[CC4] # CW725 Buttercream

[CC5] #CW625 Terracotta Canyon

[CC6] #CW810 Cherry Moon

1 set US #4 (3.5mm) straight needles

1 set US #4 (3.5mm) double-pointed needles

1 spare set of double-pointed needles, size US #4 (3.5mm) or smaller

1 E-4 (3.5mm) crochet hook

Yarn needle

Fiberfill stuffing

Small stitch holder

Safety pins

One 14" (35.5cm) Floracraft decorative foam ring (available in the floral section of craft stores)

6 small buttons

Gauge

• • •

21 stitches and 30 rows = 4" (10 cm)

••• STITCH STORY •••

M1L (Make 1 Left): Insert the left needle, from front to back, under the horizontal strand that lies between the stitch just knit and the next stitch. Knit this stitch through its back loop.

M1R (Make 1 Right): Insert the left needle, from back to front, under the horizontal strand that lies between the stitch just knit and the next stitch. Knit this stitch through its front loop.

SK2P (Slip 1, K2tog, Pass slipped stitch over): Slip the next stitch, knit 2 together, pass the slipped stitch over the stitch just worked.

GRAFTING

Place the two pieces flat with right sides up, so that the edges with live stitches are nearly touching. Position yourself so that the piece that is attached to the yarn tail is farthest from you. Thread the yarn tail onto a blunt yarn needle.

*Beginning with the stitches on the needle closest to you, insert the needle down into the first stitch, then up through the second stitch. Slide the first stitch off the needle. Working into the stitches on the needle farthest from you, insert the needle down into the first stitch, then up through the second stitch. Slide the first stitch off the needle.

Repeat from * until all stitches have been worked. Every few stitches, adjust the tension of the grafted stitches so that it matches the tension of the rest of the work.

DUPLICATE STITCH

Duplicate stitch produces the same effect of a knitted-in design by duplicating the path taken by the yarn in a knitted stitch. On the right side of the work, a knit stitch has a "V" shape. Beginning at the base of this V, bring the needle up through the work. At the top right corner of the V, bring the needle back down through the work. Bring the needle behind the work to the upper left corner of the V, and draw it up through the work. At the base of the V, bring the needle back down through the work. One duplicate stitch is complete.

I-CORD

Using a double-pointed needle, cast on 3 stitches.

Next Row: Instead of turning the work around to work back on the wrong side, slide all stitches to the other end of the needle, transfer the needle to your left hand, bring the yarn around the back of the work, and start knitting the stitches again.

Note: I-Cord is worked with the right side facing at all times.

Repeat this row to form I-cord. After a few rows, the work will begin to form a tube.

• • •

MOBILE

• • •

INCHWORM

• •

Note: The cast-on end of the worm forms its head.

Using straight needles and CC1, cast on 5 stitches.

Row 1 (RS): *K1, yo, repeat from * to last stitch, k1. 9 stitches.

Row 2 (WS): *P1, p1 tbl, repeat from * to last stitch, p1.

Row 3 (RS): K1, M1R, knit to last stitch, M1L, k1. 11 stitches.

Even-numbered Rows 4–48 (WS): Purl all stitches.

Row 5 (RS): K1, M1R, knit to last stitch, M1L, k1. 13 stitches.

Odd-numbered Rows 7–13 (RS): Knit all stitches.

Row 15 (RS): K1, ssk, knit to last 3 stitches, k2tog, k1. 11 stitches.

Rows 17 and 19 (RS): Knit all stitches.

Row 21 (RS): K1, M1R, knit to last stitch, M1L, k1. 13 stitches.

Odd-numbered Rows 23–27 (RS): Work as for Row 21. When Row 27 is complete, there are 19 stitches.

Rows 29 and 31 (RS): Knit all stitches.

Row 33 (RS): K1, ssk, knit to last 3 stitches, k2tog, k1. 17 stitches.

Odd-numbered Rows 35–39 (RS): Work as for Row 33. When Row 39 is complete, there are 11 stitches.

Rows 41 and 43 (RS): Knit all stitches.

Odd-numbered Rows 45–49 (RS): Work as for Row 33. When Row 49 is complete, there are 5 stitches.

Row 50 (WS): Purl all stitches.

Cut the yarn, leaving a tail 18" (45.5cm) long. Draw the yarn tail through the stitches on the needle, beginning with the stitch farthest from the tip of the needle. Pull tight.

Assembly

Sew together the long side edges of the piece, stuffing as you sew.

Fold the Inchworm in half so that the decrease point at the base of the head meets the corresponding point at the base of the tail. Sew these two points together along the underbelly.

Fold the head upward and sew it firmly in place.

Fold and sew the tail in the same manner.

Embroider the eyes and mouth onto the face using CC5 and CC6.

Weave in all ends.

DRAGONFLY

• •

Body

Using straight needles and CC2, cast on 5 stitches.

Purl 1 row.

Increase Row (RS): K1, M1R, knit to last stitch, M1L, k1. 7 stitches.

Repeat these 2 rows twice more. 11 stitches.

Work in stockinette stitch until the work measures 7¼" (18.5cm), ending with a wrong side row.

Decrease Row (WS): K1, ssk, knit to last 3 stitches, k2tog, k1. 9 stitches.

Purl 1 row.

Repeat these 2 rows twice more. 5 stitches.

Next Row (RS): K1, SK2P, k1. 3 stitches.

Cut the yarn, leaving a tail 18" (45.5cm) long. Draw the yarn tail through the stitches on the needle, beginning with the stitch farthest from the tip of the needle. Pull tight.

Large Wings (Make 2)

Using double-pointed needles and CC3, cast on 12 stitches. Divide stitches evenly among 3 needles and join to begin working in the round, being careful not to twist the stitches.

Knit 15 rounds.

Next Round: *Ssk, k2, k2tog, repeat from * once. 8 stitches.

Knit 1 round.

Next Round: *Ssk, k2tog, repeat from * once. 4 stitches.

Cut the yarn, leaving a tail 6" (15cm) long. Draw the yarn tail through the stitches on the needle, beginning with the first stitch in the round. Pull tight.

Draw the yarn tail to the inside of the tube and weave it in.

Small Wings (Make 2)

Using double-pointed needles and CC3, cast on 9 stitches. Divide stitches evenly among 3 needles and join to begin working in the round, being careful not to twist the stitches.

Knit 12 rounds.

Next Round: (SK2P) 3 times. 3 stitches.

Cut the yarn, leaving a 6"- (15cm-) long tail. Draw the yarn tail through the stitches on the needle, beginning with the first stitch in the round. Pull tight.

Draw the yarn tail to the inside of the tube and weave it in.

Assembly

Sew together the long side edges of the body, stuffing as you sew.

Embroider eyes onto the thicker end of the body using CC1.

Lightly stuff the wings and sew them onto the sides of the body, using the photo as a guide.

Weave in all ends.

SUN

• •

Body

Using double-pointed needles and CC4, cast on 6 stitches. Divide stitches evenly among 3 needles and join to begin working in the round, being careful not to twist the stitches.

Round 1: *K1, yo, repeat from * to end. 12 stitches.
Round 2: *K1, k1 tbl, repeat from * to end.
Round 3: Work as for Round 1. 24 stitches.
Round 4: Work as for Round 2.
Round 5: *K2, yo, repeat from * to end. 36 stitches.
Round 6: *K2, k1 tbl, repeat from * to end.
Knit 6 rounds.

Cut the yarn, and place all stitches on hold on the spare set of double-pointed needles.

Make a second piece in the same way as the first. Cut the yarn, leaving a tail approximately 30" (76cm) long.

Graft the halves of the body together, working until approximately 1" (2.5cm) is left to graft. Stuff body, and graft remaining stitches.

Sew closed the small openings at the top and bottom of the piece.

Draw the yarn tails to inside of the body.

Rays (Make 6)

Using double-pointed needles and CC5, cast on 16 stitches. Divide stitches evenly among 3 needles and join to begin working in the round, being careful not to twist the stitches.

Rounds 1–3: Knit all stitches.
Round 4: *Ssk, k4, k2tog, repeat from * once. 12 stitches.
Odd-numbered Rounds 5–9: Knit all stitches.
Round 6: *Ssk, k2, k2tog, repeat from * once. 8 stitches.
Round 8: *Ssk, k2tog, repeat from * once. 4 stitches.
Round 10: (K2tog) twice.
Bind off remaining 2 stitches.

Draw the yarn tail through the tip and to the inside of the ray. Weave the end in on the inside of the work.

Assembly

Pin the rays evenly around the perimeter of the body. Sew them in place, flaring the bottom of each so that it forms a circle.

Embroider the face using the photo as a guide and MC, CC1, and CC6.

Draw all yarn tails to the inside of the body.

LADYBUG

• •

Upper Body

Using straight needles and CC6, cast on 8 stitches.

Odd-numbered Rows 1–29: Purl all stitches.
Row 2 (RS): K3, M1L, k2, M1R, k3. 10 stitches.
Row 4 (RS): K1, M1R, knit to last stitch, M1L, k1. 12 stitches.
Row 6 (RS): K5, M1L, k2, M1R, k5. 14 stitches.
Row 8 (RS): Work as for Row 4. 16 stitches.
Row 10 (RS): K7, M1L, k2, M1R, k7. 18 stitches.
Row 12 (RS): Work as for Row 4. 20 stitches.
Row 14 (RS): K9, M1L, k2, M1R, k9. 22 stitches.

Even-numbered Rows 16–20 (RS): Knit all stitches.

Row 22 (RS): K10, M1L, k2, M1R, k10. 24 stitches.

Rows 24 and 26 (RS): Knit all stitches.

Row 28 (RS): K11, M1L, k2, M1R, k11. 26 stitches.

Row 30 (RS): Knit all stitches.

Row 31 (WS): Purl all stitches. Cut CC6.

Using MC, work as follows:

Work 2 rows in stockinette stitch.

Decrease Row (RS): K1, ssk, knit to last 3 stitches, k2tog, k1.

Purl 1 row.

Repeat these 2 rows 4 times more. 16 stitches.

Work Decrease Row.

Next Row (WS): P1, p2tog, p to last 3 stitches, p2tog tbl, p1.

Repeat these 2 rows twice more.

Bind off remaining 4 stitches.

Lower Body

Using straight needles and MC, cast on 8 stitches.

Work Rows 1–15 as for upper body.

Row 16 (RS): K10, M1L, k2, M1R, k10. 24 stitches.

Row 17 (WS): Purl all stitches.

Row 18 (RS): K11, M1L, k2, M1R, k11. 26 stitches.

Rows 19–21: Work in stockinette stitch.

Decrease Row (RS): K1, ssk, knit to last 3 stitches, k2tog, k1.

Purl 1 row.

Repeat these 2 rows 4 times more. 16 stitches.

Work Decrease Row.

Next Row (WS): P1, p2tog, p to last 3 stitches, p2tog tbl, p1.

Repeat these 2 rows twice more.

Bind off remaining 4 stitches.

Assembly

Pin upper body to lower body, easing edges to fit.

Sew edges together, stuffing body before seam is completed.

Using MC, embroider a straight line down the center of the Ladybug's back.

Using MC and duplicate stitch, sew several spots on the Ladybug's back, using the photo as a guide.

Using CC2, embroider eyes on the face.

Draw all yarn tails to the inside of the body.

BEE

• •

Body

Using a double-pointed needle and MC, cast on 3 stitches.

Work 3 rows of I-Cord.

On next row, kfb in each stitch. 6 stitches.

Divide stitches evenly between needles and join to begin working in the round.

Round 1: *K1, yo, repeat from * to end. 12 stitches.

Round 2: *K1, k1 tbl, repeat from * to end.

Round 3: *K2, yo, repeat from * to end. 18 stitches.

Round 4: *K2, k1 tbl, repeat from * to end.

Join CC4, but do not break MC.

Round 5: Using CC4, knit all stitches.

Round 6: *K3, yo, repeat from * to end. 24 stitches.

Round 7: *K3, k1 tbl, repeat from * to end.

Round 8: Using MC, knit all stitches.

Round 9: *K4, yo, repeat from * to end. 30 stitches.

Round 10: *K4, k1 tbl, repeat from * to end.

Rounds 11–13: Using CC4, knit all stitches.

Rounds 14–16: Using MC, knit all stitches.

Round 17: Using CC4, knit all stitches.

Round 18: *K3, k2tog, repeat from * to end. 24 stitches.

Round 19: Knit all stitches.

Round 20: Using MC, knit all stitches.

Round 21: *K2, k2tog, repeat from * to end. 18 stitches.

Round 22: Knit all stitches.

Round 23: Using CC4, knit all stitches.

Round 24: *K1, k2tog, repeat from * to end. 12 stitches.

Round 25: Knit all stitches. Cut CC4. Do not cut MC.

Turn body inside out through the opening between the needles, and weave in ends.
Turn body right side out and stuff.

Using MC, continue as follows:

Round 26: *K2, m1, repeat from * to end. 18 stitches.

Rounds 27–32: Knit all stitches.

Round 33: (K2tog) to end. 9 stitches.

Carefully stuff head through opening between needles.

Round 34: Knit all stitches.

Round 35: K1, (k2tog) to end. 4 stitches.

Cut the yarn, leaving a tail 6" (15cm) long. Draw the yarn tail through the stitches on the needle, beginning with the first stitch in the round. Pull tight.
Draw yarn tail to the inside of the body.

Wings (Make 2)

Using double-pointed needles and CC4, cast on 9 stitches. Divide stitches evenly among needles and join to begin working in the round, being careful not to twist the stitches.

Knit 10 rounds.

Next Round: (SK2P) 3 times. 3 stitches.

Cut the yarn, leaving a tail 6" (15cm) long. Draw the yarn tail through the stitches on the needle, beginning with the first stitch in the round. Pull tight.
Draw the yarn tail to the inside of the tube and weave it in.

Embroider eyes using CC5.

Lightly stuff the wings and sew them onto the sides body, using the photo as a guide.
Weave in all ends.

BUTTERFLY

• •

Body

Using CC6, work as for body of Dragonfly.

Wings (Make 4)

Using straight needles and CC5, cast on 20 stitches.

Row 1 (RS): Knit all stitches.

Even-numbered Rows 2–10 (WS): Purl all stitches.

Odd-numbered Rows 3–7 (RS): K1, M1R, knit to last stitch, M1L, k1. When Row 7 is complete, there are 26 stitches.

Row 9 (RS): K12, M1L, k2, M1R, k12. 28 stitches.

Row 11 (RS): K1, M1R, k12, M1L, k1. Place remaining 14 stitches on a stitch holder. There are 16 stitches on the needle.

Even-numbered Rows 12–16 (WS): Purl all stitches.

Odd-numbered Rows 13–17 (RS): K1, ssk, knit to last 3 stitches, k2tog, k1. When Row 17 is complete, there are 10 stitches.

Row 18 (WS): P1, p2tog, p to last 3 stitches, p2tog tbl, p1. 8 stitches.

Row 19 (RS): K1, ssk, knit to last 3 stitches, k2tog, k1. 6 stitches.

Row 20 (WS): P1, p2tog, p2tog tbl, p1. Bind off remaining 4 stitches.

Replace the held stitches on the needle with the right side facing, and rejoin the yarn.

Next Row (RS): K1, M1R, k12, M1L, k1. 16 stitches. Work Rows 12–20 as above.

Assembly

Sew together the long side edges of the body, stuffing as you sew.

Embroider a face onto one end of the body using the photo as a guide, using CC1, CC2, and CC5.

Sew the edges of two wing pieces together along their curved edges. Stuff gently and sew onto the side of the body. Repeat for other wing. Embroider small asterisks and flowers onto the wings using CC1 and CC2.

Weave in all ends.

MOBILE COVER

• •

Using straight needles and CC3, cast on 30 stitches. Work in stockinette stitch as follows:

*Work 20 rows using CC3.
Work 20 rows using CC6.
Work 20 rows using CC2.
Work 20 rows using CC4.
Work 20 rows using CC5.
Work 20 rows using CC1.
Repeat from * once more. Bind off all stitches.

Fold this piece in half lengthwise so the short ends meet, ensuring that the work is not twisted. Sew the short ends together and weave in ends.

Hanging Cords

Using two strands of MC held together, work a crochet chain long enough to wrap around the foam ring. Wrap the chain around the ring, insert the hook into the first stitch in the chain, and work a slip stitch to join.

Continue working the chain until it measures 9 inches from this joining point.

Cut the yarn, leaving a 5" (12.5cm) tail, but do not draw the tail through the last stitch; instead, place this stitch on hold on a safety pin.

Work two more Hanging Cords in the same way, spacing them evenly around the foam ring.

When the last chain is complete, do not cut the yarn; insert the hook into both held stitches and work a slip stitch to join them to the last stitch of the cord you just worked.

Chain 20 more stitches, then slip stitch in the stitch that joined the three cords to form a loop.

Work 25 single crochet stitches into this loop, then cut the yarn and draw it through the loop on the hook.

Weave the ends at the tops of each cord into the stitches forming the hanging loop, to strengthen the join.

Weave the ends at the base of each cord into the joining points.

Assembly

Wrap the Mobile Cover around the foam ring, so that the edges meet at the top with the hanging cords protruding. Arrange the cords and Mobile Cover so they are spaced attractively relative to each other; there will be one cord for every 2 stripes.

Use safety pins to pin the edges of the Mobile Cover together securely, ensuring that they are pinned at the points where they meet the hanging cords.

Turn the base over, so that the bottom is facing you. Mark six evenly spaced points around the bottom of ring at the intersections between stripes. These will be the points from which the creatures will hang.

Cut 6 lengths of MC, each 120" (305cm) long. At each of the points you have marked, work as follows:

Thread one length of yarn on the yarn needle. Insert the needle into the knitted fabric at the designated point and bring the yarn around the ring, beneath the fabric, back to the point where it entered; draw the yarn back out at this same point. Remove the needle and adjust so that the ends are even.

Insert the crochet hook into the fabric 2 stitches from the point where the yarn strands emerge, and pull a loop of the doubled yarn to the outside. Beginning from this loop, work a chain that is 10" (25.5cm) long. Work a slip stitch in the 9th chain stitch from the hook, and in each of the next 3 stitches.

Cut the yarn, draw it through the loop on the hook and pull tight.

Sew a button to the cord, 1" (2.5cm) above the top of the loop. Weave in ends.

Sew the edges of the Mobile Cover together, catching the hanging cords in the seam. Weave in ends.

For each creature, to find the ideal location for the hanging loop, thread a short piece of yarn through a point on the creature's back and dangle it, to see how it will hang.

Using the appropriate color for each creature, work a crochet chain 12 stitches long, then work a slip stitch in the first stitch of the chain to join it into a loop. Cut the yarn and draw the tail through the loop on the hook. Use the yarn tails to sew the loop securely to the creature, then weave them in.

To hang the creatures from the mobile, insert the loop at the base of each cord through the loop on the creature's back, and fasten the loop with the button.

• • •

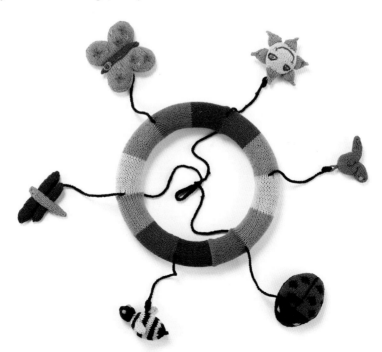

Petite Beat Bonnets

These fun and endearing vintage-inspired hats will brighten up any outfit. And, when your child is wearing one of these face-on-the-back bonnets, it will have you wondering (more than ever) if she is coming or going. Choose from four funny faces: smiling girl, wild lion, wise owl, or big-eyed alien. They all work wonders when it's time to dress a finicky kid. Just ask her if she wants to be a ferocious lion or a hooting owl—and prepare to hear compliant growls and shrieks.

DESIGNED BY KAT COYLE

Finished Sizes and Measurements

• • •

Baby (Toddler)
Shown in Toddler size

Width at widest point: 13 (15)" (33 [58]cm)

Height: 7 (8)" (18 [20.5]cm)

Materials

• • •

Tahki Stacy Charles Donegal Tweed, 100% Pure New Wool, [183yd (167m) per 100g skein], 1 skein each color

GIRL

[MC] #846 Yellow

[CC1] #896 Violet

[CC2] #810 Fuchsia

ALIEN

[MC] #803 Green

[CC] #890 Black

LION

[MC] #846 Yellow

[CC] #893 Orange

OWL

[MC] #893 Orange

[CC1] #810 Fuchsia

[CC2] #809 Turquoise

One 24" (60cm) US #7 (4.5mm) circular needle

One 24" (60cm) US #6 (4mm) circular needle

1 set US #6 (4mm) double-pointed needles (Alien only)

Stitch markers

Yarn needle

Gauge

• • •

17 stitches and 25 rows = 4" (10cm) in stockinette stitch

14 stitches and 21 rows = 4" (10cm) in loop stitch

MB (Make Bobble): (Knit into the front, then back, then front again) of the next stitch: 1 stitch increased to 3 stitches. *Turn work, k3. Turn work, p3. Repeat from * once more. Slip the second and third stitches over the first stitch. 1 stitch remains; bobble is complete.

S2KP (Slip 2, Knit 1, Pass slipped stitch over): Slip the next 2 stitches together, knitwise, as if to work a k2tog. Knit the next stitch, then pass both slipped stitches, together, over the stitch just knit. This forms a centered double decrease.

LOOP STITCH
Row 1 (RS): Knit the first stitch, but do not drop it from the left needle; bring the yarn between the needles to the front of the work, use your left thumb to hold the yarn against the front of the work, bring the yarn over your thumb and between the needles to the back of the work, making a loop approximately 1¼" (3cm) long; knit the stitch on the left needle again, and drop it from the left needle; pass the first stitch worked over the second stitch. Repeat from * for each stitch in the row.
Row 2 (WS): Purl all stitches.

DUPLICATE STITCH
Duplicate stitch produces the same effect of a knitted-in design, by duplicating the path taken by the yarn in a knitted stitch. On the right side of the work, a knit stitch has a "V" shape. Beginning at the base of this V, bring the needle up through the work. At the top right corner of the V, bring the needle back down through the work. Bring the needle behind the work to the upper left corner of the V, and draw it up through the work. At the base of the V, bring the needle back down through the work. One duplicate stitch is complete.

I-CORD
Using a double-pointed needle, cast on 4 stitches.
Next Row: Instead of turning the work around to work back on the wrong side, slide all stitches to the other end of the needle, transfer the needle to your left hand, bring the yarn around the back of the work, and start knitting the stitches again.

I-Cord is worked with the right side facing at all times. Repeat this row to form I-cord. After a few rows, the work will begin to form a tube.

• • •

BONNETS
• • •

BACK
• •

Using US #7 (4.5mm) circular needle and MC, cast on 15 (17) stitches.
Beginning with a right side row, work 6 (8) rows in stockinette stitch.

Increase Row (RS): K1, m1, knit to last stitch, m1, k1. 17 (19) stitches.
Work 7 rows in stockinette stitch.
Work Increase Row. 19 (21) stitches.
Work 13 (15) rows in stockinette stitch.

Decrease Row (RS): K1, ssk, knit to last 3 stitches, k2tog, k1. 17 (19) stitches.
Work 3 rows in stockinette stitch.

Work Decrease Row. 15 (17) stitches.
Purl 1 row.
Repeat these 2 rows twice more. 11 (13) stitches.
Cut the yarn and place the remaining stitches on hold on the US #6 (4mm) needle.

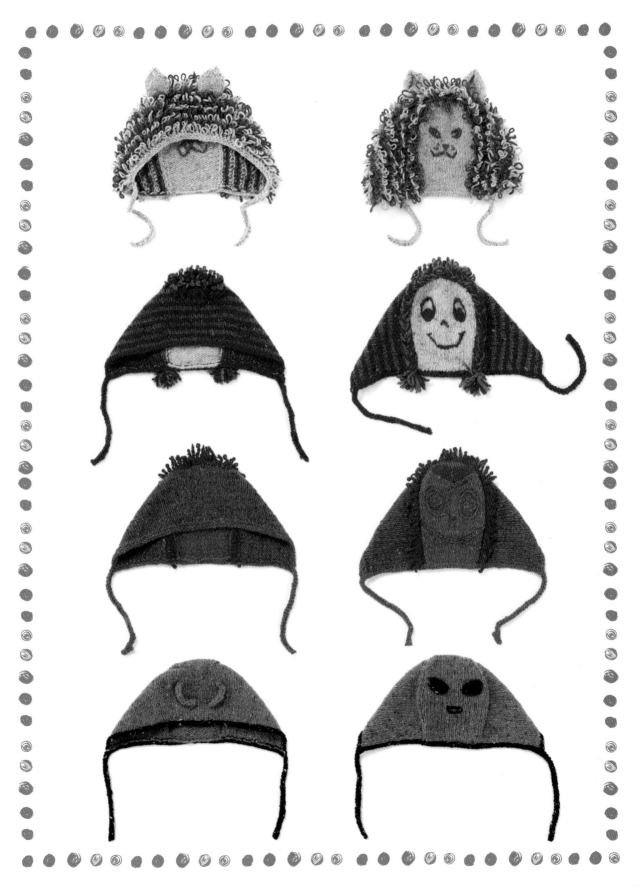

FRONT

• •

The Front is worked differently for each character.

Girl

Pick-Up Row: Using US #7 (4.5mm) circular needle and
CC1, with right side facing, pick up and knit 23 (27) stitches
along the right side edge of the Back (approximately
2 stitches for every 3 rows), place marker, work the
11 (13) held stitches along the top of the Back in loop
stitch, place marker, pick up and knit 23 (27) stitches
along the left side edge of the Back. 57 (67) stitches.
Purl 1 row.

Next Row (RS): Using CC2, knit to first marker, work
in loop stitch to second marker, knit to end.
Purl 1 row.
Work these 2 rows once more, using CC1.

Continue as follows, alternating between CC1 and
CC2 every 2 rows:

Work 0 (2) rows in stockinette stitch.

Decrease Row (RS): Knit to 2 stitches before marker,
k2tog, knit to second marker, ssk, knit to end.
Work 7 (9) rows in stockinette stitch.
Repeat these 8 (10) rows once more. 53 (63) stitches.

Work Decrease Row once more. 51 (61) stitches.
Purl 1 row.

Using CC2, knit 2 rows. Bind off all stitches purlwise.

When making Ties (See instructions in "Finishing,"
page 101), use CC2.

Lion

Note: *When working the Front for the Lion, all rows,*
including the Pick-Up Row, *are worked in loop stitch,*
unless otherwise instructed. When working the
Decrease Rows, the (ssk and k2tog) are also worked
in loop stitch.

Pick-Up Row: Using US #7 (4.5mm) circular needle
and CC, with right side facing and working all stitches
in loop stitch, pick up and work 23 (27) stitches along
the right side edge of the Back (approximately 2
stitches for every 3 rows), place marker, work the
11 (13) held stitches along the top of the Back, place
marker, pick up and work 23 (27) stitches along the
left side edge of the Back. 57 (67) stitches.
Purl 1 row.

Work 2 rows in loop stitch using MC.

Continue as follows, alternating between CC and MC
every 2 rows:

Work 2 (4) rows in loop stitch.

Decrease Row (RS): Work 1 stitch, ssk, work to 2
stitches before marker, k2tog, work to second marker,
ssk, work to last 3 stitches, k2tog, k1.
Work 3 (5) rows in loop stitch.
Repeat these 4 (6) rows once more. 49 (59) stitches.

Work Decrease Row as above. 45 (55) stitches.
Work 1 (3) rows.
Work Decrease Row once more. 41 (51) stitches.
Purl 1 row.

Using CC2, knit 2 rows (these rows are not worked in loop stitch). Bind off all stitches purlwise.

When making Ties (See instructions in "Finishing," this page), use MC.

Alien

Pick-Up Row: Using US #7 (4.5mm) circular needle and MC, with right side facing, pick up and knit 23 (27) stitches along the right side edge of the Back (approximately 2 stitches for every 3 rows), place marker, knit the 11 (13) held stitches along the top of the Back, place marker, pick up and knit 23 (27) stitches along the left side edge of the Back. 57 (67) stitches.

Work 5 (7) rows in stockinette stitch.

Decrease Row (RS): Knit to 2 stitches before marker, k2tog, knit to second marker, ssk, knit to end.
Work 7 (9) rows in stockinette stitch.
Repeat these 8 (10) rows once more. 53 (63) stitches.

Work Decrease Row once more. 51 (61) stitches.
Purl 1 row. Cut MC.

Using CC, knit 2 rows. Bind off all stitches purlwise.

When making Ties (See instructions in "Finishing," this page), use CC.

Owl

Pick-Up Row: Using US #7 (4.5mm) circular needle and CC1, with right side facing, pick up and knit 23 (27) stitches along the right side edge of the Back (approximately 2 stitches for every 3 rows), place marker, knit the 11 (13) held stitches along the top of the Back, place marker, pick up and knit 23 (27) stitches along the left side edge of the Back. 57 (67) stitches.
Purl 1 row.

Work 1 row in loop stitch.
Purl 1 row. Break CC1.

Using CC2, work 2 (4) rows in stockinette stitch.

Decrease Row (RS): Knit to 2 stitches before marker, k2tog, knit to second marker, ssk, knit to end.
Work 7 (9) rows in stockinette stitch.
Repeat these 8 (10) rows once more. 53 (63) stitches.

Work Decrease Row once more. 51 (61) stitches.
Purl 1 row. Cut CC2.

Using MC, knit 2 rows. Bind off all stitches purlwise.

When making Ties (See instructions in "Finishing," below), use MC.

Finishing

• • •

TIES

• •

Using the US #6 (4mm) circular needle and the color indicated for your creature, cast on

30 stitches; with the right side facing and continuing from the stitches on your needle, pick up and knit 17 (21) stitches along the lower edge of one side of your Bonnet, pick up and knit 15 (17) stitches along the lower edge of the Back, pick up and knit 17 (21) stitches along the lower edge of the remaining side; cast on 30 stitches. 109 (119) stitches.

Knit 1 row.
Bind off all stitches purlwise.

EMBELLISHMENT

• •

Embroider a face on the back of your Bonnet using the photos as guides, or design your own face! The Pattern for Mimi and Bobbi in At the Café contains directions for different embroidery stitches (see page 35) that may help you get started. Check suggested reading list on page 142 for additional resources.

Lion

Ears *(Make 2):*
Using US #7 (4.5mm) needle and MC, cast on 8 stitches.
Row 1 (RS): Knit all stitches.
Even-numbered Rows 2–12 (WS): Purl all stitches.
Odd-numbered Rows 3–9 (RS): K1, m1, knit to last stitch, m1, k1.
When Row 9 is complete, there are 16 stitches.

Row 11 (RS): K1, (ssk) 3 times, k2, (k2tog) 3 times, k1. 10 stitches.
Row 13 (RS): K1, (ssk) twice, (k2tog) twice, k1. 6 stitches.
Row 14 (WS): (P2tog) 3 times. 3 stitches.
Row 15 (RS): S2KP.
Cut the yarn, draw it through the remaining stitch, and pull tight.

Sew the ears to the head, approximately 2½" (6.5cm) apart, between the fourth and fifth rows of loop stitch from the back, with the wrong sides of the ears facing the back.

For the owl, the hat shown has a wide, V-shaped patch of duplicate stitch worked in CC1 at the top of the face. Instructions for duplicate stitch can be found in stitch story, page 98.

Weave in all ends.

Girl

Braids *(Make 2):*
Cut twelve 26" (66cm) strands each of CC1 and CC2. Hold the strands together so that their ends are even, and tie a piece of waste yarn around the strands at their center point. Fold the group of strands in half at this point. Divide the strands into three bundles and braid them together, tying the braid with short lengths of both colors once the braid is complete.

Sew the braids on either side of the face, covering the edge between the Front and Back of the bonnet.

Alien

Antennae *(Make 2):*
Using double-pointed needles and MC, work I-Cord for 2" (5cm).
Next Row: Continuing in I-Cord, bind off 1 stitch, MB, pass previous bound-off stitch over bobble, bind off remaining stitches.
Cut the yarn, draw it through the remaining stitch and pull tight.
Sew the antennae to the top of the hat, using the photo as a guide.

• • •

Studio Loungers

Picasso wore pants much like this pair when he was relaxing beachside in the south of France. Your little leisure artist will enjoy lounging in them, too. Just roll up the cuffs and let him enjoy all those lazy summer day activities, from drawing on the pavement with chalk to making paintings of the ocean and all its wildlife. The pants are knit from side to side so that the self-striping yarns create these jaunty vertical stripes.

DESIGNED BY KAT COYLE

Finished Sizes and Measurements

• • •

6–12 months (12–18 months, 18–24 months)
Shown in size 18–24 months

Waist Circumference
(after elastic insertion):
17½ (17¾, 18)" (44.5 [45, 45.5]cm)

Hip Circumference: 23 (23, 25)"
(58.5 [58.5, 63.5]cm)

Length: 16½ (18, 19)" (42 [45.5, 48.5]cm)

Materials

• • •

4 (4, 5) balls Filatura Di Crosa Porto Cervo Print, 100% Cotton, [88yd/80m per 50g])
Color: #505 Blue Print

1 US #8 (5 mm) circular needle, 24" (60cm) or longer

1 set US #8 (5mm) double-pointed needles

Yarn needle

1 package ¾" (20mm) waistband elastic

Sewing needle and thread

Safety pins or split-ring markers

Gauge

• • •

17 stitches and 24 rows = 4" (10cm)
in stockinette stitch

••• STITCH STORY •••

These pants are worked in stockinette stitch, with a garter stitch hem and a reverse stockinette stitch waistband casing. The front and back pieces are cast on along their long side edges, and are worked lengthwise. The crotch and inner leg shaping are worked through the use of short rows and consecutive bind-offs. When casting on and binding off, leave long yarn tails to use when seaming the pants.

Note that the measurements shown in the schematic are for each piece, before seaming, and include the unfolded waistband casing. The finished measurements listed on page 103 are for the pants after seaming.

WRAP AND TURN

Note: Used when working short rows.

To wrap and turn on a RS row, knit to point specified in pattern, bring yarn to front of work between needles, slip next stitch to right-hand needle, bring yarn around this stitch to back of work, slip stitch back to left-hand needle, and turn work to begin purling back in the other direction.

To wrap and turn on a WS row, purl to point specified in pattern, bring yarn to back of work between needles, slip next stitch to right-hand needle, bring yarn around this stitch to front of work, slip stitch back to left-hand needle, turn work to begin knitting back in the other direction.

WORKING WRAPS TOGETHER
WITH WRAPPED STITCHES

When you encounter a wrapped stitch, work the wraps together with the stitches they wrap as follows:

When working a RS row, knit to wrapped stitch. Slip next stitch from left needle to right needle, use tip of left needle to pick up wrap and place it on right needle, insert left needle into both wrap and stitch, and knit them together.

When working a WS row, purl to wrapped stitch. Slip next stitch from left needle to right needle, use tip of left needle to pick up wrap and place it on right needle, slip both wrap and stitch back to left needle, and purl together through back loops.

I-CORD

Using a double-pointed needle, cast on 3 stitches.

Next Row: Instead of turning the work around to work back on the wrong side, slide all stitches to the other end of the needle, transfer the needle to your left hand, bring the yarn around the back of the work, and start knitting the stitches again.

Note: I-Cord is worked with the right side facing at all times.

Repeat this row to form I-cord. After a few rows, the work will begin to form a tube.

• • •

PANTS

• • •

RIGHT BACK

• •

Using the circular needle, cast on 75 (81, 85) stitches.

Row 1 (WS): K3, purl to last 5 stitches, k5.

Row 2 (RS): P5, knit to end.

Repeat these 2 rows 14 (14, 15) times more, then work Row 1 once more. 31 (31, 33) rows have been worked; the work measures 5¼ (5¼, 5½)" (13.2 [13.2, 14]cm).

Shape Inner Leg and Crotch

Row 1 (RS): Bind off 16 stitches, knit to end. 59 (65, 69) stitches.

Row 2 (WS): Purl all stitches.

Row 3 (RS): Bind off 5 stitches, knit to end. 54 (60, 64) stitches.

Row 4 (WS): Purl all stitches.

Row 5 (RS): Bind off 4 stitches, k38 (44, 48) (39 [45, 49] stitches on right needle), wrap and turn. Purl to end. 50 (56, 60) stitches.

Row 6 (RS): Bind off 4 stitches, k24 (28, 31) (25 [29, 32] stitches on right needle), wrap and turn. Purl to end. 46 (52, 56) stitches.

Row 7 (RS): Bind off 4 stitches, k9 (13, 15) (10 [14, 16] stitches on right needle), wrap and turn. Purl to end. 42 (48, 52) stitches.

Row 8 (RS): Bind off 2 stitches, k4 (6, 7) (5 [7, 8] stitches on right needle), wrap and turn. Purl to end. 40 (46, 50) stitches.

Bind off all stitches. As you work the bind-off row, when you come to a wrapped stitch, pick up the wrap and knit it together with the stitch it wraps.

LEFT BACK

• •

Using the circular needle, cast on 75 (81, 85) stitches.
Row 1 (WS): K5, purl to last 3 stitches, k3.
Row 2 (RS): Knit to last 5 stitches, p5.
Repeat these 2 rows 15 (15, 16) times more. 32 (32, 34) rows have been worked; the work measures 5¼ (5¼, 5½)" (13.2 [13.2, 14]cm).

Shape Inner Leg and Crotch
Row 1 (WS): Bind off 16 stitches, purl to end. 59 (65, 69) stitches.
Row 2 (RS): Knit all stitches.
Row 3 (WS): Bind off 5 stitches, purl to last 3 stitches, k3. 54 (60, 64) stitches.
Row 4 (RS): Knit all stitches.

Row 5 (WS): Bind off 4 stitches, p38 (44, 48) (39 [45, 49] stitches on right needle), wrap and turn. Knit to end. 50 (56, 60) stitches.
Row 6 (WS): Bind off 4 stitches, p24 (28, 31) (25 [29, 32] stitches on right needle), wrap and turn. Knit to end. 46 (52, 56) stitches.
Row 7 (WS): Bind off 4 stitches, p9 (13, 15) (10 [14, 16] stitches on right needle), wrap and turn. Knit to end. 42 (48, 52) stitches.
Row 8 (WS): Bind off 2 stitches, p4 (6, 7) (5 [7, 8] stitches on right needle), wrap and turn. Knit to end. 40 (46, 50) stitches.

Bind off all stitches. As you work the bind-off row, when you come to a wrapped stitch, pick up the wrap and purl it together with the stitch it wraps.

RIGHT FRONT

• •

Using the circular needle, cast on 75 (81, 85) stitches.
Row 1 (WS): K5, purl to last 5 stitches, k3.
Row 2 (RS): Knit to last 5 stitches, p5.
Repeat these 2 rows 12 (12, 13) times more, then work Row 1 once more.

Next Row (RS): Knit to last 8 stitches, yo, k2tog, k1, p5. Work 4 more rows in pattern. 32 (32, 34) rows have been worked; the work measures 5¼ (5¼, 5½)" (13.2 [13.2, 14]cm).

Shape inner leg and crotch as for Left Back.

LEFT FRONT

• •

Using the circular needle, cast on 75 (81, 85) stitches.
Row 1 (WS): K3, purl to last 5 stitches, k5.
Row 2 (RS): P5, knit to end.
Repeat these 2 rows 12 (12, 13) times more, then work Row 1 once more.

Next Row (RS): P5, k1, ssk, yo, knit to end.
Work 3 more rows in pattern. 31 (31, 33) rows have been worked; the work measures 5¼ (5¼, 5½)" (13.2 [13.2, 14]cm).

Shape inner leg and crotch as for Right Back.

DRAWSTRINGS

• •

Work 2 pieces of I-Cord, each 10" (25.5cm) long.

Finishing

• • •

Immerse all pieces in lukewarm water and allow them to soak until they are thoroughly saturated. Gently squeeze out the water (do not wring!) and lay the pieces on top of several towels on a flat surface. Carefully pin them out to the dimensions given. Allow them to dry completely.

Sew the Right Front and Right Back together along their long side edges. Sew the Left Front and Left Back together in the same way. Sew each leg together along the inseam edges.

Sew the Back pieces together along the shaped crotch edges, then sew the Front pieces together in the same way, leaving the top 5 stitches (the reverse stockinette stitch waistband elastic casing) unsewn.

The fold line for the waistband casing is the division between the stockinette and reverse stockinette sections at the waist edge of the pants. Fold the casing along this line to the inside of the work and sew the edge in place. To be sure the seam is straight, use pins or waste yarn to mark the stitching line, which is the fifth column of stitches from the fold line.

Cut a piece of waistband elastic that is 18½ (18¾, 19)" (47 [47.5, 48.5]cm) long, or 1" (2.5cm) longer than the desired waistband measurement. Insert the elastic into the casing, ensuring that it does not twist. Overlap the ends of the elastic by 1" (2.5cm), and sew the ends together securely.

Pull the elastic out of the casing by about 6" (15cm) on one side. Sew one end of one Drawstring securely to the elastic about 5" (12.5cm) from the center front, on the side of the elastic that faces the front of the pants. Thread the other end of the Drawstring through one eyelet at the center front of the elastic casing, so that it emerges at the front of the pants.

Repeat this for the other Drawstring, on the other side of the Pants. Tie a knot in the end of each Drawstring.

Sew the elastic casing closed.
Weave in all ends and gently press seams.

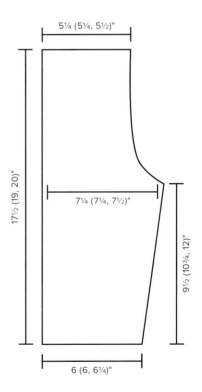

5¼ (5¼, 5½)"

17½ (19, 20)"

7¼ (7¼, 7½)"

9½ (10¾, 12)"

6 (6, 6¼)"

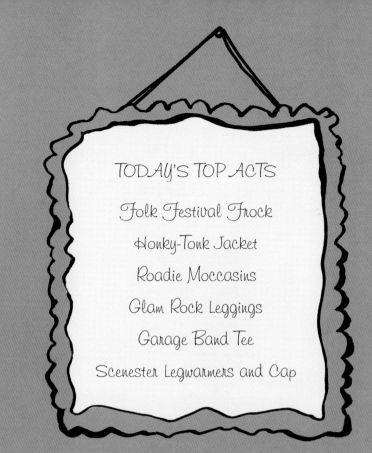

TODAY'S TOP ACTS

Folk Festival Frock

Honky-Tonk Jacket

Roadie Moccasins

Glam Rock Leggings

Garage Band Tee

Scenester Legwarmers and Cap

At the Concert

Get your ticket to the concert: It's rocking with high-energy togs for little musicians and their fans. Choose from a Honky-Tonk Jacket or Glam Rock Leggings, a Garage Band Tee or a Folk Festival Frock—whatever the style, there's a project that matches your baby's beat. So, get your yarn out and knit to the rhythm. The groove factor is high, the beat is on, and the kids are always hopping.

Folk Festival Frock

This freewheeling frock features soft pink and brown stripes and a sweet pinafore style. It's easy to knit up for your favorite flower child or folkie. She can pair it with tights and a turtleneck in cold weather, but when it gets warm, she can just throw on the dress and go. I can see her now, twirling to the music, barefoot and happy!

DESIGNED BY EDNA HART

••• STITCH STORY •••

When working the stripe patterns in this dress, carry the yarns not in use loosely along the side of the work when working back and forth, or the inside of the work when working in the round.

Bodice Stripe Pattern

Rows 1–2: Work in stockinette stitch using MC.
Rows 3–6: Work in stockinette stitch using CC1.
Rows 7–8: Work in stockinette stitch using MC.
Rows 9–12: Work in stockinette stitch using CC2.
Repeat these 12 rows for bodice stripe pattern.

Finished Sizes and Measurements
• • •

1 (2, 3, 4) years
Shown in size 2 years

Chest: 18 (21, 23½, 25½)" (45.5 [53.5, 59.5, 64.8]cm)

Skirt Circumference: 25½ (29¾, 33, 36)" (64.8 [75.5, 84, 91]cm)

Length: 16 (18, 21, 23)" (40.5 [45.5, 53.5, 58.5]cm)

Materials
• • •

Manos del Uruguay Cotton Stria [100% Cotton; 116 yd/106 m per 50g skein]; 1 skein each color

[MC] #220 Brown

[CC1] #214 Light Pink

[CC2] #292 Magenta

One 16" (40cm) US #6 (4mm) circular needle

1 US #8 (5mm) circular needle, 16" (40cm) or 24" (60cm)

1 C-2 (2.75mm) crochet hook

Stitch marker

Yarn needle

Gauge
• • •

17 stitches and 26 rows = 4" (10cm) in stockinette stitch using US #6 (4mm) needle

16 stitches and 24 rows = 4" (10cm) in stockinette stitch using US #8 (5mm) needle

Skirt Stripe Pattern

Rounds 1–7: Knit all stitches using CC1.
Rounds 8–9: Knit all stitches using MC.
Rounds 10–16: Knit all stitches using CC2.
Rounds 17–18: Knit all stitches using MC.
Repeat these 18 rounds for skirt stripe pattern.

• • •

DRESS

• • •

STRAPS

• •

Using the US #8 (5mm) needle and CC2 (CC2, MC, MC), cast on 8 (9, 10, 11) stitches.

Sizes 1 year and 2 years only:
Beginning with a right side row, work 2 rows in stockinette stitch, then proceed to directions below.

All Sizes:
Beginning with a right side row, work in stockinette stitch as follows:
Work 2 rows using MC.
Work 2 rows using CC1.
Work 2 rows using MC.
Work 2 rows using CC2.

Repeat these 8 rows 3 times more. 34 (34, 32, 32) rows have been worked.

Sizes 3 years and 4 years only:
Work 2 rows using MC.
Work 2 rows using CC1.
Work 2 rows using MC.
38 rows have been worked.

All Sizes:
Cut the yarn and place all stitches on a stitch holder. Make a second strap in the same way, but do not cut the yarn, and leave the stitches on the working needle.

BODICE FRONT

• •

Next Row (RS): Using CC2, knit all stitches on the needle, cast on 16 (18, 20, 22) stitches, knit the held stitches of the first strap. 32 (36, 40, 44) stitches.

Work 1 (1, 3, 3) more rows using CC2.

Work 12 (14, 16, 18) rows in bodice stripe pattern. (You will have just completed 4 [2, 2, 4] rows using CC2 [MC, CC1, CC1].)
Cut the yarn and place all stitches on a stitch holder.

BODICE BACK

• •

Lay the work flat with the right side up, with the held stitches nearest you and the cast-on ends of the straps farthest from you. Using the US #8 (5mm) needle and CC2, pick up and knit 1 stitch in each cast-on stitch of the strap on your right, cast on 16 (18, 20, 22) stitches, pick up and knit 1 stitch in each cast-on stitch of the remaining strap. 32 (36, 40, 44) stitches.

Work as for the Bodice Front, but do not cut the yarn, and leave the stitches on the working needle.

LOWER BODICE

• •

Next Row (RS): Continuing in bodice stripe pattern, knit all stitches of the Bodice Back, cast on 4 (6, 7, 7) stitches, knit the held stitches of the Bodice Front, cast on 4 (6, 7, 7) stitches. 72 (84, 94, 102) stitches. Place a marker and join to begin working in the round, ensuring that the cast-on underarm stitches are not twisted.

Work 11 (15, 19, 23) rounds in bodice stripe pattern. You will have just completed a 4-round stripe using CC2 (CC1, CC2, CC1).

SKIRT

• •

Round 1: Using the US #6 (4mm) needle and MC, *k2tog, yo, repeat from * to end.
Round 2: Using MC, knit all stitches.
Round 3: Using CC1 (CC2, CC1, CC2), k1, *m1, k2, repeat from * to last stitch, m1, k1. 108 (126, 141, 153) stitches. This is Round 1 (10, 1, 10) of skirt stripe pattern.

Continue working in skirt stripe pattern until the Skirt measures 9 (10, 11, 12)" (23 [25.5, 28, 30.5]cm).

Bind off all stitches using one strand of each color held together.

Finishing

• • •

Using CC2, work 1 round of single crochet around the armhole and neckline edges.
Weave in all ends.

Immerse the dress in lukewarm water and allow it to soak until it is thoroughly saturated. Gently squeeze out the water (do not wring!) and lay the dress on top of several towels on a flat surface. Carefully pin it out to the dimensions given. Allow it to dry completely.

Drawstring
Cut 2 strands each of MC, CC1, and CC2, each approximately 40 (44, 48, 50)" (101.5 [112, 122, 127]cm) long. Knot all strands together at one end.

Holding each pair of like-colored strands together as one, make a braid approximately 28 (32, 35, 37)" (71 [81, 89, 94]cm) long. Knot the ends together and trim.

Weave the drawstring through the eyelets at the waist.

• • •

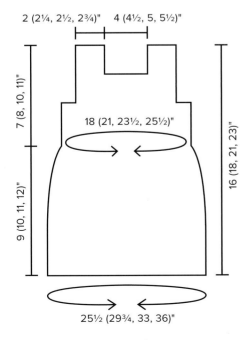

Honky-Tonk Jacket

This faux-suede jacket is a simple knit worked in stockinette stitch with garter edges and modified drop sleeves. Toggle buttons and fringe trimming give it a down-home country feel. Your little folk cowboy or -girl will love to wear it for impromptu yodeling sessions or just for strolling around town. Why not go all out and pair it with boots and a stetson hat?

DESIGNED BY MARY-HEATHER COGAR

••• STITCH STORY •••

SELVEDGE STITCHES
When working this pattern, slip the first stitch of each row purlwise. This will give a smooth edge to the knitted pieces, which will make seaming easier. It will also create a nicer-looking front edge for the cardigan.

CONTRASTING BAND
Using CC, knit 3 rows, beginning with a right side row. Purl 1 row.
Knit 2 rows. You will have a narrow band of CC, with a garter stitch ridge running along the upper and lower edges. Cut CC.

Finished Sizes and Measurements

• • •

6–12 months, (1–2 years, 2–3 years, 3–4 years)
Shown in size 1–2 years

Chest: 20 (22, 24, 25)" (51 [56, 61, 63.5]cm)

Length: 11 (13, 13, 14)" (28 [33, 33, 35.5]cm)

Materials

• • •

Yarn: Berroco Suede, 100% Nylon, [120yd (111m) per 50g ball]

[MC] #3714 Hopalong Cassidy; 3 (3, 4, 5) balls

[CC] #3717 Wild Bill Hickock; 1 ball

1 set US #7 (4.5mm) straight needles

1 set US #6 (4mm) straight needles

1 US D-3 (3.25mm) crochet hook

Four ¾" (20mm) brown toggle buttons

Split-ring markers or safety pins

Stitch holders

Yarn needle

Gauge

• • •

20 stitches and 27 rows = 4" (10 cm) in stockinette stitch, using US #7 (4.5mm) needles

THREE-NEEDLE BIND-OFF

Hold both pieces of knitting with right sides together. Insert needle into the first stitch on the front needle and first stitch on the back needle, and knit them together. *Repeat this for the next stitch on the front and back needles. Draw the first stitch worked over the second stitch.*
Repeat from * to * until all stitches have been bound off. Cut the yarn and draw it through the remaining stitch.

• • •

JACKET
• • •
BACK
• •

Using MC and US #6 (4mm) needles, cast on 52 (56, 62, 64) stitches.

*Work 4 rows in garter stitch.

Using US #7 (4.5mm) needles and beginning with a right side row, work in stockinette stitch until the work measures 5½ (6¾, 6½, 6¾)" (14 [17, 16.5, 17]cm), ending with a wrong side row.

Work Contrasting Band (see pattern notes, page 115). Do not cut MC; carry MC loosely along side of work while working the Band.

Work 2 rows in stockinette stitch using MC. The work measures 6½ (7¾, 7½, 7¾)" (16.5 [19.7, 19, 19.7]cm).*

Shape Armholes
Bind off 3 (3, 3, 4) stitches at the beginning of the next 2 rows. 46 (50, 56, 56) stitches remain.

Work in stockinette stitch until the work measures 11 (13, 13, 14)" (28 [33, 33, 35.5]cm). Place all stitches on a stitch holder.

RIGHT FRONT
• •

Using MC and US #6 (4mm) needles, cast on 27 (29, 32, 33) stitches.
Work as for the Back from * to *.
K 1 row.

Shape Armhole
Next Row (WS): Bind off 3 (3, 3, 4) stitches, purl to end. 24 (26, 29, 29) stitches remain.

Continue in stockinette stitch until work measures 9 (11, 11, 11½)" (23 [28, 28, 29.2]cm), ending with a right side row.

Shape Neckline
Next Row (WS): Sl 1, p17 (17, 20, 20); slip the remaining 6 (8, 8, 8) to a stitch holder.

Decrease Row 1 (RS): Sl 1, k2tog, knit to end.

Decrease Row 2 (WS): Sl 1, purl to last 3 stitches, p2tog, p1.

Repeat these 2 rows twice more. 12 (12, 15, 15) stitches.

Sizes 2–3 years and 3–4 years only:

Work Decrease Row 1 once more. 14 stitches.

All Sizes

Continue in stockinette stitch until the work measures 11 (13, 13, 14)" (28 [33, 33, 35.5]cm). Cut the yarn, leaving a 36" (91cm) tail. Place all stitches on a stitch holder.

LEFT FRONT

• •

Using MC and US #6 (4mm) needles, cast on 27 (29, 32, 33) stitches.

Work as for the back from * to *.

Shape Armhole

Next Row (RS): Bind off 3 (3, 3, 4) stitches, knit to end. 24 (26, 29, 29) stitches.

Continue in stockinette stitch until the work measures 9 (11, 11, 11½)" (23 [28, 28, 29.2]cm), ending with a wrong side row.

Shape Neckline

Next Row (RS): Sl 1, k17 (17, 20, 20); slip the remaining 6 (8, 8, 8) to a stitch holder.

Decrease Row 1 (WS): Sl 1, p2tog tbl, purl to end.

Decrease Row 2 (RS): Sl 1, knit to last 3 stitches, ssk, k1.

Repeat these 2 rows twice more. 12 (12, 15, 15) stitches.

Sizes 2–3 years and 3–4 years only:

Work Decrease Row 1 once more. 14 stitches.

All Sizes

Continue in stockinette stitch until the work measures 11 (13, 13, 14)" (28 [33, 33, 35.5]cm). Cut the yarn, leaving a 36" (91cm) tail. Place all stitches on a stitch holder.

SLEEVES (MAKE 2)

• •

Using MC and US #6 (4mm) needles, cast on 36 (41, 44, 46) stitches.
Work 4 rows in garter stitch.

Using US #7 (4.5mm) needles and beginning with a right side row, work 6 (8, 8, 4) rows in stockinette stitch.

Increase Row (RS): Sl 1, k1, m1, knit to last 2 stitches, m1, k2.
Work 5 (5, 7, 7) rows in stockinette stitch.
Repeat these 6 (6, 8, 8) rows 3 (4, 4, 6) times more, then work Increase Row once more. 46 (53, 56, 62) stitches.

Continue in stockinette stitch until the work measures 5¾ (7¼, 8¾, 9¾)" (14.5 [18.5, 22.2, 24.8]cm), ending with a wrong side row.

Work Contrasting Band.

Work 4 rows in stockinette stitch using MC. The work measures 7 (8½, 10, 11)" (18 [21.5, 25.5, 28]cm).
Loosely bind off all stitches.

Finishing

• • •

SHOULDER SEAMS

• •

With the right side of the Back facing, slip the first 12 (12, 14, 14) stitches at the right edge of the piece to a US #6 (4mm) needle. Slip the held shoulder stitches of the Right Front to a second US #6 (4mm) needle. With a US #7 (4.5mm) needle and the yarn tail attached to the Front, join the Front and Back at the right shoulder using a three-needle bind-off.

Join the left shoulder seam in the same way.

COLLAR

• •

Using MC and US #6 (4mm) needles, with the right side facing, knit the held stitches of the Right Front neckline, pick up and knit 3 stitches for every 4 rows along the Right Front neckline edge, knit the held

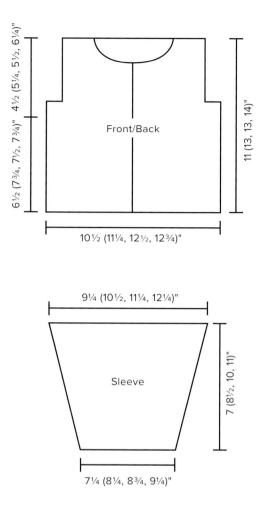

stitches of the Back neckline, pick up and knit 3 stitches for every 4 rows along the Left Front neckline edge, knit the held stitches of the Left Front neckline.

Work 4 rows in garter stitch.

Using US #7 (4.5mm) needles, continue in garter stitch until the collar measures 1¾ (2, 2, 2¼)" (4.5 [5, 5, 5.5]cm).
Bind off all stitches very loosely.

ASSEMBLY

• •

Sew the bound-off edge of one Sleeve to the vertical edge of one armhole, matching the center of the Sleeve to the end of the Shoulder Seam. Sew the top portion of the Sleeve to the bound-off edges of the armhole, then sew the Sleeve seam and side seam. Repeat for the remaining Sleeve and side.

TOGGLE LOOPS

• •

Use split-ring markers or safety pins to mark desired locations for four toggle loops. (Place the loops along the right front edge for a girl, or the left front edge for a boy.)

Insert the crochet hook into the front edge of the sweater at the desired location of a loop. Use a slip stitch to attach MC to the sweater. Chain 8, then slip stitch in the sweater, close to the first slip stitch. Cut the yarn and draw it through the loop on the hook. Pull tight.

Repeat for the other 3 loops.

Sew the toggles to the other front edge, opposite the loops.

Weave in all ends.

FRINGE

• •

Cut lengths of CC as follows: fifteen pieces 11" (28cm) long, twelve pieces 9" (23cm) long, and sixty-six pieces 7" (18cm) long.

The Fringe will be attached at points along the center of the Contrasting Band as follows:
With the right side facing, at the desired point, insert the crochet hook into the work so that the hook enters the work above a stitch and emerges below that stitch.

Hold three strands of yarn together and fold them approximately in half to form a loop. Use the hook to grab this loop, and draw it through the fabric.

When approximately ½" (1.5cm) of the loop has been pulled through the fabric, without removing the hook from the loop, use the hook to grab the loose ends of the strands of yarn and pull them through the loop. Pull tight to fasten.

Attach one cluster of 11" (28cm) strands on either side of the front opening of the jacket, one at the center back, and one on each side of the center back.
Attach one cluster of 9" (30.5cm) strands next to each cluster of 11" (28cm) strands (except for the cluster at center back).
Attach two clusters of 7" (18cm) strands next to each cluster of 9" (30.5cm) strands, and seven clusters, evenly spaced, on each Sleeve.

• • •

Roadie Moccasins

Baby moccasins worked in the same faux suede as the Honky-Tonk Jacket (page 115) are perfect for taking your little one on the road. The sculptural shaping used to make these socks gives the simple stitchwork a lot of texture. Chocolate brown embroidery is added to imitate traditional lacing.

DESIGNED BY MARY-HEATHER COGAR

Finished Sizes and Measurements

• • •

0–3 months (3–6 months, 6–9 months, 9–12 months)
Shown in size 3–6 months

Foot length: 2¼ (2¾, 3, 3¼)" (6 [7, 7.5, 8.25]cm)

Materials

• • •

Berroco Suede, 100% Nylon, [120yd (111m) per 50g ball], 1 ball each color

[MC] #3714 Hopalong Cassidy

[CC] #3717 Wild Bill Hickock

1 set of 5 US #7 (4.5mm) double-pointed needles
Yarn needle

Gauge

• • •

20 stitches and 27 rows = 4" (10 cm) in stockinette stitch

• • • STITCH STORY • • •

GARTER IN THE ROUND (LEG SECTION)
Round 1: Knit
Round 2: Purl
Repeat these two rounds for pattern.

• • •

MOCCASIN BOOTIES

• • •

SOLE

• •

Note: The Sole is worked back and forth on two needles.
Using CC, cast on 4 (6, 8, 10) stitches.
Knit 2 rows.
Next Row: K1, kfb, knit to last 2 stitches, kfb, k1. 6 (8, 10, 12) stitches.

Work 12 (14, 16, 18) rows in garter stitch.
Next Row: K1, ssk, knit to last 3 stitches, k2tog, k1.
Knit 1 row.
Bind off remaining 4 (6, 8, 10) stitches purlwise.

FOOT

• •

Note: Stitches for the bootie are picked up around the perimeter of the sole using double-pointed needles, then the lower part of the foot is worked in the round. While stitches are being picked up, the needles will be designated needle 1, needle 2, etc.

Using MC and needle 1, pick up and knit 12 (14, 16, 18) stitches along side edge of sole (1 stitch in the edge of each garter ridge along one long, straight edge); using needle 2, pick up and knit 1 stitch in the rounded corner of the sole, pick up and knit 1 stitch in each cast-on or bound-off stitch (depending on which end you are at), and 1 stitch in the next rounded corner (6 [8, 10, 12] stitches on needle 2); using needle 3, pick up and knit 12 (14, 16, 18) stitches along the side edge of the sole (as for needle 1); using needle 4, pick up and knit stitches in the rounded corners and along the remaining edge of the sole (as for needle 2).

12 (14, 16, 18) stitches each on needles 1 and 3; 6 (8, 10, 12) stitches each on needles 2 and 4. 36 (44, 52, 60) stitches in total.

Join to begin working in the round and knit 4 (4, 6, 6) rounds.

INSTEP

• •

Rounds 1 & 2: Knit to last 2 stitches on needle 1, k2tog; ssk, knit to last 2 stitches on needle 2, k2tog; ssk, knit to end of needle 3; knit all stitches on needle 4. When Round 2 is complete, there are 10 (12, 14, 16) stitches each on needles 1 and 3, 2 (4, 6, 8) stitches on needle 2, and 6 (8, 10, 12) stitches on needle 4. 28 (36, 44, 52) stitches.

Round 3: Knit to last 2 stitches on needle 1, k2tog; knit all stitches on needle 2; ssk, knit to end of needle 3; knit all stitches on needle 4.

Round 4: Knit to last 2 stitches on needle 1, k2tog; knit all stitches on needle 2; ssk. Do not complete round.

Slip last stitch from needle 1 and first stitch from needle 3 to needle 2. There are 7 (9, 11, 13) stitches each on needles 1 and 3, 4 (6, 8, 10) stitches on needle 2, and 6 (8, 10, 12) stitches on needle 4. 24 (32, 40, 48) stitches.
Turn work so that the wrong side of the work on needle 2 is facing.

Work the stitches on needle 2 back and forth in short rows, as follows:
Row 1 [WS]: Sl 1, purl to last stitch on needle 2, p2tog (last stitch on needle 2 purled together with first stitch on needle 1).
Row 2 [RS]: Sl 1, knit to last stitch on needle 2, ssk (last stitch on needle 2 worked together with first stitch on needle 3).
Repeat these 2 rows 2 (4, 4, 6) times more. 4 (4, 6, 6) stitches each remain on needles 1 and 3.

Knit to end of needle 3; k1, k2tog, knit to last 3 stitches on needle 4, ssk, k1. There are 4 (4, 6, 6) stitches each on needles 1 and 3, and 4 (6, 8, 10) stitches each on needles 2 and 4. 16 (20, 28, 32) stitches.

LEG

• •

Knit 4 rounds.
Work 8 rounds in garter stitch.
Bind off all stitches very loosely. (You may wish to use a larger needle to bind off.)

Finishing

• • •

Using one strand of CC and yarn needle, embroider x-shaped stitches along "seams" formed by short-row shaping (see photos). Work blanket stitch around edge of cuff. See suggested reading list and websites on page 142 for resources.

Weave in ends.

• • •

Glam Rock Leggings

Your little rock 'n' roller will look the part in these fitted leggings conveniently designed to fit over standard diapers. The Op Art checks are created in stranded knitting worked flat; the legs are sewn along the inseam and a snappy back gusset is inserted. Pair with a simple white or black onesie for a mod outfit.

DESIGNED BY BETH ABARAVICH

Finished Size and Measurements

• • •

6–12 months

Waistband circumference: 16½" (42cm)

Circumference of pants below waistband: 20" (51cm)

Length: 15" (38cm)

Materials

• • •

Rowan Wool Cotton, 50% Merino Wool / 50% Cotton, [123yd (113m) per 50g ball]

[MC] #908 Inky; 2 balls

[CC] #900 Antique; 1 ball

1 set US #3 (3.25mm) straight needles

1 set US #5 (3.75mm) straight needles

Smooth waste yarn, of a heavier weight than the working yarn

Yarn needle

Gauge

• • •

25 stitches and 27 rows = 4" (10cm) in stranded color pattern using US #5 (3.75mm) needles

These pants are knit in a stranded color pattern. Two colors of yarn are used in each row, with the color not in use carried loosely across the back of the work. The chart shows which stitches are to be worked in which colors.

1x1 rib (Worked over an even number of stitches)
Row 1 (RS): *K1, p1, repeat from * to last 2 stitches, k2.
Row 2 (WS): P2, *k1, p1, repeat from * to end.
Repeat these 2 rows for 1x1 rib.

• • •

BABY LEGGINGS
• • •

LEFT LEG
• •

Using US #5 (3.75mm) needles and MC, cast on 48 stitches.
Work 8 rows in 1x1 rib.
Work Rows 1–82 of Left Leg chart (page 126), increasing and binding off as indicated.
When Row 82 is completed, there are 50 stitches.
Place all stitches on hold on waste yarn.

RIGHT LEG
• •

Work as for the Left Leg, except work from the Right Leg chart (page 127).

BACK GUSSET
• •

Using US #5 (3.75mm) needles and MC, cast on 3 stitches.

Purl 1 row.
Increase Row (RS): K1, m1, knit to last stitch, m1, k1.
Repeat these 2 rows twice more. 9 stitches.

Work 3 rows in stockinette stitch.
Work Increase Row as above.
Repeat these 4 rows twice more. 15 stitches.

MC
CC
M Make 1
⊠ Bind off 1 stitch

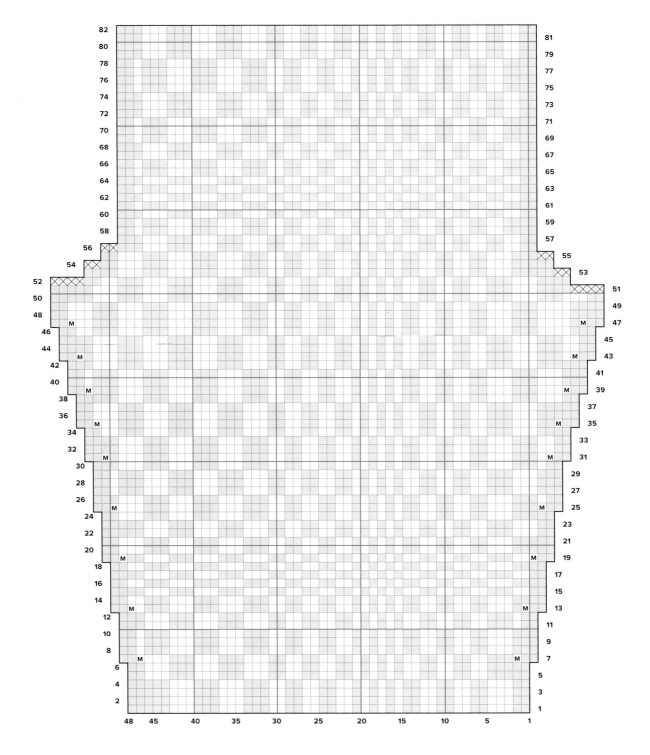

RIGHT LEG

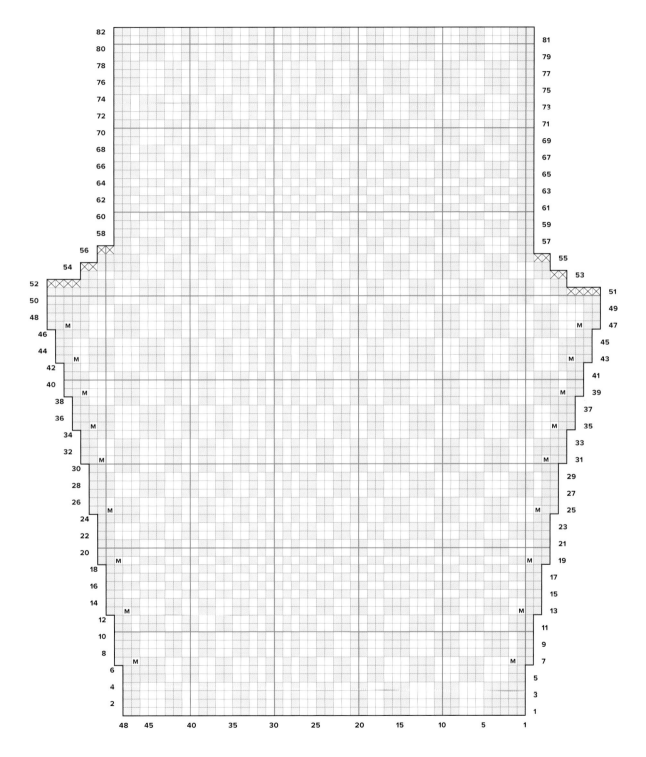

Work 10 rows in 1x1 rib using US #3 (3.25mm) needles, decreasing 1 stitch in the first row. 120 stitches. Bind off all stitches loosely in pattern.

ASSEMBLY

• • •

Sew the side edges of the Back Gusset to the adjacent edges of each Leg.

Sew the Legs together at the center front.
Sew the inseams.
Weave in all ends.

• • •

Purl 1 row.
Work Increase Row as on page 125.
Repeat these 2 rows twice more. 21 stitches.

Continue in stockinette stitch until the work measures 5½" (14cm) when measured down the center.
Place all stitches on hold on waste yarn.

Finishing

• • •

Immerse all pieces in lukewarm water and allow them to soak until thoroughly saturated. Gently squeeze out the water (do not wring!) and lay the pieces on top of several towels on a flat surface. Carefully pin them out to the dimensions given. Allow them to dry completely.

WAISTBAND

• • •

Place all pieces on a US #3 (3.25mm) needle with right sides facing; place the Left Leg at the back end of the needle, the Back Gusset next to the Left Leg, then the Right Leg next to the Back Gusset, at the working end of the needle. Reattach MC.

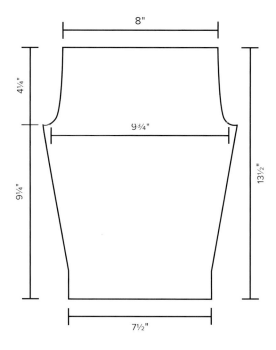

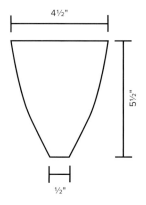

Garage Band Tee

Worked in fine easy-care cotton, this classic raglan tee is a great project for knitters who like working at a small gauge. The pattern features carefully conceived details for an authentic look, including folded hems and a contrasting neckline and three-quarter-length sleeves. With its graphic "01" logo you can tell your junior rock star he's number one. Add a pair of blue jeans and some sneakers and he's ready to roll.

DESIGNED BY MARY-HEATHER COGAR

• • • STITCH STORY • • •

INTARSIA

The number motif on the front of this sweater is worked using the intarsia technique. To work a motif using this technique, work each area of color from a separate strand of that color. The yarn not in use is not stranded across the back of the work.

To prepare for working an intarsia design, wind a few small balls or bobbins of each color.

Finished Sizes and Measurements
• • •

6–12 months (1–2 years, 2–3 years, 3–4 years)
Shown in 1–2 years size

Chest: 23½ (24, 24¾, 25½)"
(57.2 [61, 62.8, 63.5]cm)

Length: 11½ (13¼, 13¾, 14)"
(28.5 [33.5, 35, 35.5]cm)

Materials
• • •

Brown Sheep Cotton Fine, 80% Cotton / 20% Wool, [222yd (203m) per 50g skein]

[MC] #CW201 Barn Red; 2 (2, 3, 3) skeins

[CC] #CW585 Wolverine Blue; 1 (1, 2, 2) skeins

1 pair US #2 (2.75mm) straight needles

One 16" (40cm) US #2 (2.75mm) circular needle or size needed to achieve gauge

Bobbins

Stitch markers

Stitch holder

Yarn needle

Gauge
• • •

28 stitches and 41 rows = 4" (10cm) in stockinette stitch

Note: Gauge given is measured after swatch has been machine washed in cold water and dried on very low heat. The gauge of a fabric worked in this yarn will change considerably after washing and drying. Please take the time to wash and dry the swatch to ensure that the shirt will fit after it has been washed!

When you come to a point in the pattern where you need to change colors, drop the old color and pick up the strand of the new color from underneath the old color, so that the strands are twisted at the point where the two colors meet. This will prevent holes from forming at these points.

Check suggested reading list and websites on page 142 for resources.

• • •

TEE
• • •

BACK
• •

Hem
Using MC, cast on 83 (85, 87, 89) stitches. Beginning with a right side row, work 5 rows in stockinette stitch.

Next Row (WS): Knit all stitches. This row forms a turning ridge for the hem.

Work 6 rows in stockinette stitch.

Fold the hem facing along the turning ridge to the inside of the work. The wrong sides of the hem facing and hem are together, and the cast-on edge is directly behind the stitches on the needle. In the next row, you will join the hem and hem facing.

Next Row (RS): *Insert the tip of the left needle into the outside edge of the stitch of the cast-on edge which is directly behind the first stitch on the needle. Knit this stitch together with the first stitch on the needle. Repeat from * until all stitches have been worked.

Lower Body
Work 60 (70, 74, 74) rows in stockinette stitch, ending with a right side row.

Raglan Shaping
Bind off 4 stitches at the beginning of the next 2 rows. 75 (77, 79, 81) stitches.

Work 2 rows in stockinette stitch.
Decrease Row 1 (WS): P2, p2tog, purl to last 4 stitches, p2tog tbl, p2.
Work 2 rows in stockinette stitch.
Decrease Row 2 (RS): K2, ssk, knit to last 4 stitches, k2tog, k2.
Repeat these 6 rows 5 (8, 8, 9) times more. 51 (41, 43, 41) stitches.

Size 6–12 months only:
Purl 1 row.
Work Decrease Row 2 as above.
Repeat these 2 rows 7 times more. 35 stitches.

Size 2–3 years only:
Work 2 rows in stockinette stitch.
Work Decrease Row 1 as above.
Knit 1 row.

All Sizes:
Bind off all stitches.

FRONT
• •

Cast on and work hem as for the Back.
Work 57 (67, 71, 71) rows in stockinette stitch, ending with a wrong side row.

Next Row (RS): K28 (29, 30, 31), place marker, work Row 1 of the chart over the next 26 stitches, place marker, k29 (30, 31, 32).
From this point, work the stitches between markers following the chart on page 132.

Work 2 rows in stockinette stitch, ending with a right side row.

Raglan and Neckline Shaping
Work raglan shaping as for the Back. At the same time, work neckline shaping as follows.

Once all 29 rows of the chart have been worked, ending with a right side row, work 5 (5, 9, 11) rows using MC only, without removing markers.

RINGER TEE CHART

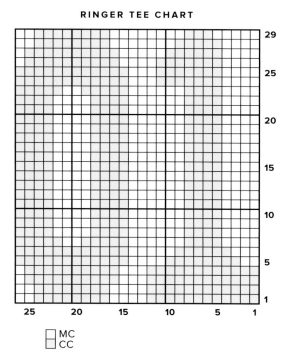

☐ MC
☐ CC

Next Row (RS): Work to first marker, remove marker, k6 (4, 4, 4). With a new ball of yarn, k15 (19, 19, 19) and place these stitches on a stitch holder; work to the end of the row using the new ball of yarn, removing the remaining marker.

You have just placed the center 15 (19, 19, 19) stitches on hold, and have two sets of stitches on the needle, each attached to a separate ball of yarn. These two sets of stitches are worked at the same time. While shaping the neckline following the directions below, continue working raglan shaping as set.

Row 1 (WS): Work to last 4 stitches of first set of stitches, p2tog tbl, p2; purl first 2 stitches of second set of stitches, p2tog, work to end of second set of stitches.

Row 2 (RS): Work to last 4 stitches of first set of stitches, k2tog, k2; knit first 2 stitches of second set of stitches, ssk, work to end of second set of stitches. Repeat these 2 rows 2 (3, 3, 3) times more.

Size 6–12 months only:
Work Row 1 as above, once more.

All Sizes:
Continue working without further shaping at the neckline edges until all raglan shaping is complete. Bind off the remaining 3 stitches in each set of stitches.

SLEEVES (MAKE 2)
• •

Using CC, cast on 46 (50, 50, 52) stitches. Work hem as for the Back.

Work 9 (3, 5, 9) rows in stockinette stitch, ending with a wrong side row.

Increase Row (RS): K1, m1, knit to last stitch, m1, k1. Work 11 (9, 9, 9) rows in stockinette stitch.
Repeat these 12 (10, 10, 10) rows 2 (4, 5, 5) times more. 52 (60, 62, 64) stitches.

Knit 1 row.

Raglan Shaping

Bind off 4 stitches at the beginning of the next 2 rows. 44 (52, 54, 56) stitches.

Work 2 rows in stockinette stitch.
Decrease Row 1 (WS): P2, p2tog, purl to last 4 stitches, p2tog tbl, p2.
Work 2 rows in stockinette stitch.
Decrease Row 2 (RS): K2, ssk, knit to last 4 stitches, k2tog, k2.
Repeat these 6 rows 5 (2, 4, 4) times more. 20 (40, 34, 36) stitches.

Purl 1 row.
Work Decrease Row 2 as above.
Repeat these 2 rows 7 (17, 13, 14) times more.
Bind off the remaining 4 (4, 6, 6) stitches.

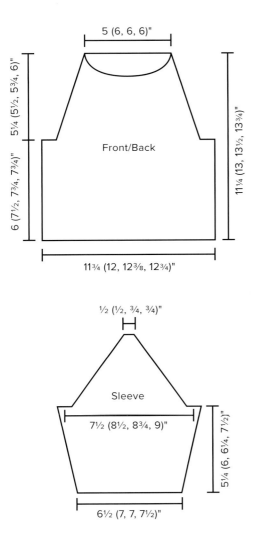

5 (6, 6, 6)"

5¼ (5½, 5¾, 6)"

Front/Back

11¼ (13, 13½, 13¾)"

6 (7½, 7¾, 7¾)"

11¾ (12, 12⅜, 12¾)"

½ (½, ¾, ¾)"

Sleeve

7½ (8½, 8¾, 9)"

5¼ (6, 6¼, 7½)"

6½ (7, 7, 7½)"

Finishing

• • •

Sew the Sleeves to the Front and Back along the bound-off underarm stitches and raglan edges.

COLLAR

• •

With the right side facing, using the circular needle and CC and beginning at the right back raglan seam, pick up and knit 1 stitch in each bound-off stitch along the back neckline edge, pick up and knit 1 stitch in each bound-off stitch and in each row to the held stitches at the center front neckline, knit these held stitches, pick up and knit 1 stitch in each row and in each bound-off stitch to the right back raglan seam. Join to begin working in the round. Be sure you have an even number of stitches; if you do not, decrease an extra stitch when working the next round.

When working the next round, decrease 1 stitch at each raglan seam.

Next Round: *K1, p1, repeat from * to end.
Repeat this round 4 times more.
Bind off all stitches very loosely in pattern.

Weave in all ends.
Wash and dry sweater gently (see note, page 129 for instructions).

Scenester Legwarmers and Cap

Featuring stripes, stripes, and more stripes, these playfully mismatched legwarmers and caps will inspire your small gamine to dance to the beat of her own drum. Two patterns make a pair and three colorways are shown, so knitting these is a free-for-all. You'll have plenty of yarn to complete a pair of legwarmers and a cap, but if you're knitting the larger sizes, you may need to do a little juggling, swapping out the main colors for some of the lesser used ones.

DESIGNED BY KAT COYLE

Finished Sizes and Measurements

• • •

6–12 months (1–2 years, 2–4 years)

LEGWARMERS

Circumference: 6 (7½, 9½)"
(15 [19, 24]cm)

Length: 8¼ (10, 13)" (21 [25.5, 33]cm)

CAPS

Circumference: 16 (17½, 19)"
(40.5 [44.5, 48.5]cm)

Materials

• • •

Rowan Wool Cotton, 50% Merino Wool, 50% Cotton [123yd (113m) per 50g ball; 1 ball each color

Note: *1 ball of each color will be enough to make a pair of legwarmers and a hat. However, if you are making the largest size, you will need to change which colors are the dominant colors (MC, CC1, and CC2) and which are the accent colors (CC3 and CC4) between pieces.*

COLORWAY A

[MC] #965 Mocha

[CC1] #910 Gypsy

[CC2] #930 Riviera

[CC3] #951 Tender

[CC4] #907 Deepest Olive

COLORWAY B

[MC] #962 Pumpkin

[CC1] #946 Elf

[CC2] #959 Bilberry Fool

[CC3] #901 Citron

[CC4] #955 Ship Shape

COLORWAY C

[MC] #943 Flower

[CC1] #963 Smalt

[CC2] #952 Hiss

[CC3] #951 Tender

[CC4] #910 Gypsy

1 set US #4 (3.5mm) straight needles

1 set US #5 (3.75mm) straight needles

Yarn needle

Gauge

• • •

22 stitches and 30 rows = 4" (10cm) in stockinette stitch using US #5 (3.75mm) needles

Some rows on these accessories are knit in a stranded color pattern. When two colors of yarn are used in a row, the color not in use is carried loosely across the back of the work. The chart shows which stitches are to be worked in which colors.

When switching colors between rows, if a color is used often, carry it loosely along the side of the work instead of cutting and reattaching it.

When working from the charts, some rows are repeated. Because of this, the row numbers in the charts will not correspond to the number of rows you have worked.

All charts begin on a right side row.

For a mismatched pair of legwarmers as shown, work one legwarmer from Legwarmer Chart 1, and one from Legwarmer Chart 2.

1X1 RIB
Note: Worked over an even number of stitches.
Row 1 (RS): *K1, p1, repeat from * to last 2 stitches, k2.
Row 2 (WS): P2, *k1, p1, repeat from * to end.
Repeat these 2 rows for 1x1 rib.

• • •

LEGWARMERS
• • •

Using US #4 (3.5mm) needles and the color of the first row of the chart you have chosen, cast on 34 (42, 52) stitches. Work the first 8 rows of the chart in 1x1 rib.

Using US #5 (3.75mm) needles, work in stockinette stitch, repeating rows as indicated, until you have completed chart row 40 of Legwarmer Chart 1, or chart row 44 of Legwarmer Chart 2.
54 (68, 90) rows have been worked.

Using US #4 (3.5mm) needles, work the last 8 rows of the chart in 1x1 rib. Bind off all stitches loosely in pattern. Cut the yarn, leaving a 18" (45.5cm) tail.

COLORWAY A

Chart 1   Chart 2

COLORWAY B

Chart 1   Chart 2

COLORWAY C

Chart 1   Chart 2

LEGWARMER CHART 1

Row	
48	
46	
44	
42	
40	Work these rows 1 (2, 3) times
38	
36	
34	
32	Work these rows 3 (4, 5) times
30	These rows worked for size 2–4 years only
28	
26	
24	These rows worked for size 6–12 months only
22	
20	Work these rows 3 (5, 8) times
18	
16	Work these rows 1 (2, 3) times
14	
12	
10	Work these rows 3 (4, 5) times
8	
6	
4	
2	

LEGWARMER CHART 2

Row	
52	
50	
48	
46	
44	
42	
40	
38	Work these rows 2 (3, 4) times
36	
34	Work this row 1 (1, 7) times
32	Work this row 1 (3, 3) times
30	
28	Work these rows 1 (2,4) times
26	
24	
22	
20	Work these rows 2 (3, 5) times
18	
16	
14	Work these rows 2 (3, 4) times
12	
10	
8	
6	
4	
2	

Legend:

- ☐ MC
- ▨ CC1
- ⊠ CC2
- ◯ CC3
- • CC4

- ☐ Repeat as indicated
- ☐ These rows are not worked for all sizes

CAP

• • •

Using US #4 (3.5mm) needles and the color of the first row of the chart you have chosen, cast on 88 (96, 104) stitches.

Work the first 8 rows of the chart in 1x1 rib.

Using US #5 (3.75mm) needles, work in stockinette stitch, repeating rows as indicated, until you have worked 38 (48, 48) rows.

You will have just worked chart row 26 of Cap Chart 1, or chart row 32 of Cap Chart 2.

Continue working from the Chart, while shaping the crown of the Cap as follows:

Row 1 (RS): *K6, k2tog, repeat from * to end. 77 (84, 91) stitches.

Even-numbered Rows 2–12 (WS): Purl all stitches.

Row 3 (RS): *K5, k2tog, repeat from * to end. 66 (72, 78) stitches.

Row 5 (RS): *K4, k2tog, repeat from * to end. 55 (60, 65) stitches.

Row 7 (RS): *K3, k2tog, repeat from * to end. 44 (48, 52) stitches.

Row 9 (RS): *K2, k2tog, repeat from * to end. 33 (36, 39) stitches.

Row 11 (RS): *K1, k2tog, repeat from * to end. 22 (24, 26) stitches.

Row 13 (RS): (K2tog) to end. 11 (12, 13) stitches.

Row 14 (WS): (P2tog) 5 (6, 6) times, p1 (0, 1).

Cut the yarn, leaving a 12" (30.5cm) tail, and draw it through the remaining 6 (6, 7) stitches. Pull tight.

Finishing
• • •
Weave in all ends, except for the long tails left when binding off.

Immerse all pieces in lukewarm water and allow them to soak until thoroughly saturated. Gently squeeze out the water (do not wring!) and lay the pieces on top of several towels on a flat surface. Allow them to dry completely.

Use the yarn tails to sew up the side edges of each piece, and weave in these ends.
• • •

CAP CHART 1

CAP CHART 2

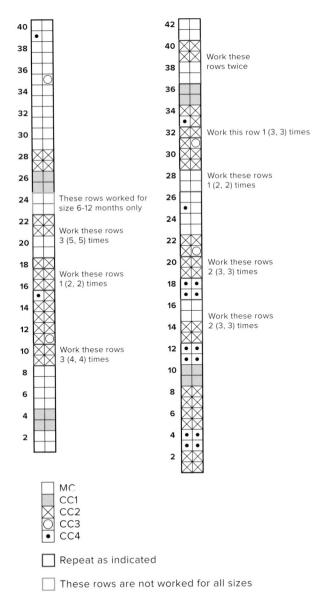

These rows worked for size 6-12 months only

Work these rows 3 (5, 5) times

Work these rows 1 (2, 2) times

Work these rows 3 (4, 4) times

Work these rows twice

Work this row 1 (3, 3) times

Work these rows 1 (2, 2) times

Work these rows 2 (3, 3) times

Work these rows 2 (3, 3) times

MC
CC1
CC2
CC3
CC4

Repeat as indicated

These rows are not worked for all sizes

MEET THE BOHO BABIES

AIDAN

BECKETT

CARLOTTA

DAISY

DASHIELL

DEXTER

ESME

ISAIAH

JADEN

MADELEINE

MADISON

MIA

NONA

REESE

TANNER

VIVIAN

MEET THE DESIGNERS

• • •

Beth Abaravich learned how to knit while studying at the Art Institute of Chicago. After attending Otis College of Art and Design's fashion program in Los Angeles, she worked as a fashion designer for Bob Mackie. Most recently, Beth worked at the Knit Cafe on Melrose Avenue and has designs featured in the store's book, *Greetings from Knit Café*.

Mary-Heather Cogar is a California Institute of the Arts graduate living in Los Angeles, where she wishes for more rainy days. Her work is featured in several craft books, including *Greetings from Knit Café*, the *Crochet Pattern A Day Calendar*, and *Creative Pincushions*. She sews, embroiders, knits, crochets, spins yarn, designs, and sells her handmade creations and patterns—and blogs about it all—at www.rainydaygoods.com.

Kat Coyle is a knitwear designer whose work has been published in *Knit Wit* by Amy R. Singer, *Lace Style* by Pam Allen, and *Greetings from Knit Café* by Suzan Mischer. Her designs have also been featured in the magazines *Interweave Knits*, *Knitscene*, and *Knitty* (knitty.com). She lives in Los Angeles.

Edna Hart is a longtime knitter and the proprietress of a funky boutique in the Silver Lake neighborhood of Los Angeles. In an earlier incarnation, she was a hard-working costume designer in the film world. Now she entertains her many loyal customers with her quick wit and endearing sensibilities. See more of her eclectic goodies at her website: www.ednahartboutique. blogspot.com.

Julia Trice lives in southern California with her loving husband and animal menagerie. An attorney by day, in her spare time she handles her knitting needles with authority and dabbles in knitwear design. Julia's designs have been published online and in print, most recently in *Greetings from Knit Café*. Her popular blog, Mind of Winter (http://mindofwinter.prettyposies.com/) captures her astute observations on life and knitting.

The multitalented and tech-savvy **Marnie MacLean** is a creative powerhouse. She recently moved to Oregon with her beloved dog Panda and boyfriend Leo. Delve deeper into her knitting know-how by browsing her website, http://marniemaclean.com, which is full of informative tutorials on all things fiber and sparkles with Marnie's personality.

ACKNOWLEDGMENTS

• • •

I am very lucky to have the support of my family and friends who are always there when I need help or advice. Much of their wisdom was needed during the creation of this book. Thanks to Johnny for keeping the house in order and for cooking when I forgot to eat! Kisses to Felix for being so funny and keeping me laughing even when I hadn't slept.

I'm grateful to Amy Singer for creating Knitty.com and changing my knitting life, and to Jillian Moreno and Kristi Porter for their spark and invitation to work on this project. Kristi was also kind enough to proofread the book with a sharp eye.

Thank you Beth, Mary-Heather, Edna, Julia, and Marnie, the talented knitwear designers who contributed patterns; they inspire me with their artistry.

Many thanks to the yarn companies who generously supplied all the yarn we used to make the samples in this book: Berroco, Blue Sky Alpacas, Brown Sheep Company, Cascade Yarns, Crystal Palace Yarns, Filatura de Crosa, Louet, Manos del Uruguay Design Source, Rowan, Tahki/Stacy Charles, and Trendsetter Yarns.

This dream came true because of the team of people at Potter Craft, who have so skillfully published and promoted the book, especially Rosy Ngo, for signing up *Boho Baby Knits*, and Isa Loundon, for making sure it all came off without a hitch.

Many thanks to the folks at Quirk Packaging for putting everything together so beautifully—the wonderful, creative publisher Sharyn Rosart; my editor, Sarah Scheffel, for making sure that my words made sense and for so much more; Lynne Yeamans, for her great design and baby wrangling at the photo shoot; and stylist Janet Prusa, for her chic taste and her skills as a baby wrangler, too. And thank you, Marion Vitus, for the fun illustrations of favorite baby hangouts.

Big thanks to charming Mandy Moore for being the tech editor—not only is she good with figures, she is also a night owl (like me).

Three cheers to Frank Heckers for his luminous photographs filled with warmth and magic.

Thank you, thank you to all the little models whose super-cuteness makes me very happy and brings all the designs to life.

YARN SOURCES

• • •

The yarns used in this book are widely available everywhere. We've offered this guide to help you locate a store nearest you.

Berroco, Inc.
14 Elmdale Road
PO Box 367
Uxbridge, MA 01569
508-278-2527
www.berroco.com

Blue Sky Alpacas, Inc.
PO Box 88
Cedar, MN 55011
888-460-8862
www.blueskyalpacas.com

Brown Sheep Company, Inc.
100662 County Road #16
Mitchell, NE 69357
800-826-9136
www.brownsheep.com

Cascade Yarns
1224 Andover Park East
Tukwila, WA 98188
800-548-1048
www.cascadeyarns.com

Crystal Palace Yarns
Straw Into Gold, Inc.
160 23rd Street
Richmond, CA 94804
510-237-9988
www.straw.com

Filatura di Crosa
Distributed by Tahki •
Stacy Charles, Inc.
See contact information below.

Louet North America
3425 Hands Road
Prescott, ON, Canada K0E 1T0
613-925-4502
www.louet.com

Manos del Uruguay
Design Source
PO Box 770
Medford, MA 02155
888-566-9970
www.manos.com.uy

Rowan
Distributed by Westminster Fibers, Inc.
4 Townsend West, Unit 8
Nashua, NH 03063
800-445-9276
www.knitrowan.com

Tahki • Stacy Charles, Inc.
70-30 80th Street, Building 36
Ridgewood, NY 11385
800-338-YARN
www.tahkistacycharles.com

Trendsetter Yarns
16745 Saticoy Street #101
Van Nuys, CA 91406
818-780-5497
www.trendsetteryarns.com

USEFUL BOOKS AND WEBSITES

• • •

To learn more about knitting techniques (from basic to advanced), knitted embellishments, and embroidery, check out these sources.

Brown, Nancy. *The Crocheter's Companion* (The Companion Series). Interweave Press, 2002.

Epstein, Nicky. *Nicky Epstein's Knitted Embellishments: 350 Appliqués, Border Cords, and More!* Interweave Press, 1999.

Fassett, Kaffe. *Kaffe Fassett's Pattern Library: Over 19 Creative Knitwear Designs.* The Taunton Press, 2003 (originally published in the United Kingdom by Ebury Press, Random House, 2003).

Manning, Tara Jon. *Nature Babies: Natural Knits and Organic Crafts for Moms, Babies, and a Better World.* Potter Craft, 2006.

Nicholas, Kristin. *Colorful Stitchery: 65 Hot Embroidery Projects to Personalize Your Home.* Storey Publishing, 2005.

Righetti, Maggie. *Knitting in Plain English.* St. Martin's Griffin, 2007.

Stanley, Montse. *Reader's Digest Knitter's Handbook: A Comprehensive Guide to the Principles of Handknitting.* Reader's Digest, 1999.

Vogue Knitting: The Ultimate Knitting Book. Sixth & Spring Books, 2002 (originally published by Pantheon, 1989).

www.knitting.about.com
www.knittinghelp.com
www.knitty.com
www.learntoknit.com
www.techknitting.blogspot.com

INDEX

· · ·